Sultanahmet and Süleymaniye

Ahmet Vefa Çobanoğlu

Tarkan Okçuoğlu

SCALA

First published in Turkey by
Scala Yayıncılık
Ankara Cad. No. 107 Hoşağası Han, Dük. 78
Cağaloğlu, Istanbul, Turkey

First published in the rest of the world by
Scala Publishers Ltd, Northburgh House,
10 Northburgh Street, London EC1V OAT

ISBN (Turkey): 978-605-88606-7-4
ISBN (rest of the world): 978 1 85759 629 8

Editor: Brian Johnson
Copy Editors: Malcolm Imrie, Zoe Charteris
Design, map and plans: Murat Celep, Deney Design Ltd, Istanbul
Printed in Turkey

10 9 8 7 6 5 4 3 2 1

Front cover and flap: The mosque of Sultan Ahmed; stained glass window near
the *mihrap*.
Back cover and flap: The Süleymaniye; calligraphy in a pendentive.
Page 1: Polychrome painting in a pendentive at the mosque of Sultan Ahmed.
Page 4: North portal of the Süleymaniye mosque, view from the forecourt.
Pages 60: Minaret and forecourt of the mosque of Sultan Ahmed.

Illustration credits:
Levent Karaoğlu: All photos except those listed below.
Alp Alper: front cover, back cover, pp. 62, 70–1, 85.
Erdal Yazıcı: pp. 10–11, 14, 44 (left), 47, 51.
Galeri Alfa, Istanbul: pp. 8, 13, 38–39, 65, 67, 68.
Deutches Archäologisches Institut (DAI), Istanbul: pp. 9, 59, 66, 102.
Topkapı Sarayı Müzesi, Istanbul: p. 52.
Österreichische Nationalbibliothek, Vienna: p. 6 (below).
Chester Beatty Library, London: pp. 43, 44–5.
Courtesy of Lütfi Bayer, Istanbul: p. 78 (left).
Courtesy of Sinan Ceco, Istanbul: p. 76, 97, 101.

Editor's Note:
All quotations from the Qur'an are from Marmaduke Pickthall's English
translation, *The Glorious Qur'an*, London, 1930; repr. Istanbul, 1996.

Contents

Süleymaniye

The Mosque and Complex of Sultan Süleyman I

Tarkan Okçuoğlu

The Süleymaniye, the mosque and complex of buildings (*külliye*) erected by Sultan Süleyman I (*r.* 1520–66), crowns one of Istanbul's seven hills and commands a superb view of the Golden Horn. Besides a majestic place of worship, it includes schools, a hospital, soup kitchen, hospice and bath, as well as the tombs of the sultan, his wife and other members of the Ottoman family.

It was the custom of Ottoman sultans to build mosques in their names with the wealth gained from victorious military campaigns. After the conquest of Istanbul in 1453, the edifices they endowed grew in size and grandeur. Istanbul's first big *külliye* was built between 1463 and 1470 to honour Fatih, 'the Conqueror', Sultan Mehmed II (*r.* 1444–6 and 1451–81). A mosque lay at the centre of this complex, and eight theological schools, or *medreses*, flanked it on the east and west. Mausoleums, a library, hospice, hospital, caravanserai, market and bath were constructed near the schools. The *medreses* served as Istanbul's first comprehensive educational institutions in the Ottoman period. They were erected on level terrain, in a symmetrical pattern resembling renaissance architecture, with spaces between them for students to spend time outside. The *külliye* of Fatih established a brand new urban space.

Sultan Süleyman the Magnificent, or Kanuni, 'the Lawgiver', as he is known to Turks, carried out more than ten military campaigns during his forty-six year reign. He extended the borders of the Ottoman Empire in all directions of the compass, to Hungary and to Georgia, and to Algeria, Ethiopia and Yemen. The seventeenth-century Turkish traveller Evliya Çelebi (1611–82) recounted that the Süleymaniye was built with spoils from victories at Belgrade, Rhodes and Malta (1565).

Mimar Sinan (*c.* 1490–1588), the chief Ottoman court architect, planned and supervised the construction of the Süleymaniye, which would reflect the strength and splendour of the Ottoman state. An engineer of consummate skill with a careful attention to detail, he had already erected a *külliye* for Süleyman in memory of the sultan's son, Mehmed, who had

BELOW
Sultan Süleyman I (*r.* 1520–66).

died at a young age in 1543. This complex, the *külliye* of Şehzade, 'the Prince', was located roughly half way between the *külliye* of Fatih and another complex, built by the Conqueror's successor, Bayezid II (*r.* 1481–1512).

Fourteen years later, and almost ninety years after the *külliye* of Fatih had been erected, Süleyman witnessed the completion of a mosque in his own name in Istanbul. He was in the thirty-seventh year of his reign when it opened in 1557. Henceforth, this mosque would be the focal point of one of the most important religious and social facilities, both in the capital and in the Ottoman world.

Location and Surroundings

The summit of Istanbul's third hill, overlooking the Golden Horn, was chosen as the site for the Süleymaniye. On one side, it was adjacent to the Eski Saray, or Old Palace, the first of the great Ottoman residences in the city (built by Mehmed II near today's Beyazıt Square). By the sixteenth century, the palace served solely as living quarters for the women of the sultans. Constructed out of wood, it had extensive gardens, some of which were annexed to the area of the new complex. No trace of this residence remains today. In the nineteenth century, the headquarters of the Ministry of War of the Ottoman Empire was erected on its former site (today part of Istanbul University).

The administrative centre of the Janissary corps, the most elite unit in the Ottoman army, was situated on the other side of the tract of land selected for the Süleymaniye (where the office of the Istanbul Mufti now stands). A number of large commercial buildings occupied the surrounding district, which was a lively hub of trade, extending down to the port on the Golden Horn.

Layout of the Mosque and Complex
See the plan on the inside front cover

The Süleymaniye mosque and its dependencies top one of Istanbul's hills, as do Hagia Sophia and the Bayezid and Fatih mosques. All the buildings in the complex are arranged geometrically around the mosque; however, the plan does not display the strict symmetry of the *külliye* of Fatih, mainly because of the irregular topography. The Süleymaniye was built on sloping terrain that required extensive terracing.

A primary school for young boys (*sıbyan mektebi*), two *medreses* – the first (*evvel*) and second (*sani*) – and a medical school (*tıp medresesi*) are situated on the west side of the mosque. The façades of these buildings, which formerly housed shops in their lower archways, face the mosque across a plaza, known

as Tiryaki Çarşısı, or Theriac (Antidote) Market. Today, coffee houses and restaurants occupy these commercial spaces where, among other items, medicinal opium was once sold.

A hospital (*darüşşifa*) stands to the north of the mosque, directly across from the medical school. Students at the school served as interns in the hospital. A soup kitchen, or *imaret*, of the highest quality (*darüzziyafe*), and a hospice (*tabhane*) are also located to the north of the mosque. Side by side, they combined the functions of feeding and housing the poor. These buildings were constructed on terraces and with high retaining walls to adapt to the grade of the hillside and remain level with the mosque's courtyard. Their substructures housed stables and a caravanserai.

On the east side of the mosque, two more *medreses* – the third (*salis*) and fourth (*rabi*) – are perched on the slope that descends sharply to the Golden Horn. The topography required that their inner courtyards be built in step-like fashion on an incline, shored up with a series of compartments below. A separate school of *hadis* (Ar. *hadith,* traditions related to the Prophet Muhammed), the *darülhadis*, lies to the southeast of the mosque, flanking a street known as Dökmeciler Caddesi, or Avenue of the Metal Workers, after a nearby market for metalware. Its rooms are at an angle to the mosque's outer precinct, and beneath them, shops open onto the street. The mosque's bath, the former Dökmeciler Hamamı, is located a short distance away from these structures, in the direction of the Golden Horn.

A cemetery occupies the court behind the mosque (to the south), which includes the mausoleum (*türbe*) of Süleyman, as well as that of his wife Hürrem Sultan. The sultan's tomb is aligned exactly with the *kıble* (the direction of Mecca, towards which Muslims pray). Behind these funerary monuments is a

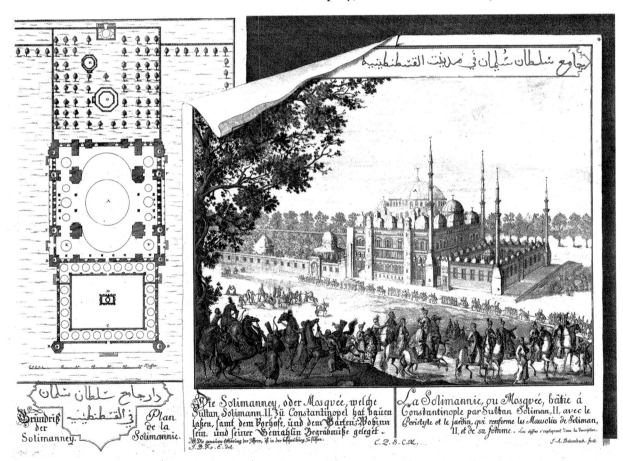

RIGHT
The inner courtyard, or 'white harem', and its domed arcade.

OPPOSITE
The rectangular ornamental fountain at the centre of the inner court was compared to the grottoes of Naples by one sixteenth-century European traveller.

small building for the caretaker of the mausoleums (*türbedar odası*), which also served as a Qur'an readers' room. During the eighteenth and nineteenth centuries this cemetery became a popular burial place for the Ottoman elite.

An inscription on the main entrance to the Süleymaniye mosque's prayer hall indicates that construction began in June of 1550 and finished in October 1557, but excavation and the laying of the foundations commenced before that. Mimar Sinan was responsible for the entire project, including the choice of

the site. He prepared detailed plans and a scale model, which guided the work from the outset.

According to Melchior Lorichs (1527–*c*. 1588), a Danish artist attached to an embassy sent to the Ottoman court by Holy Roman Emperor Ferdinand I in 1555, the mosque was inaugurated on 4 October 1557 – with all the considerable pomp and splendour that the sultan could muster, attended by every person in the court. Süleyman presented the key of the mosque to Sinan, with the words: 'It is worthy that you above all should open this mosque, the fruit of your loyalty, honesty and prayer'.

Years later, Sinan referred to the Süleymaniye mosque as his journeyman work. He considered the Selimiye mosque, built later in Edirne, to be his masterpiece.

Over time, legends emerged about the construction of the Süleymaniye mosque. In the seventeenth century, Evliya Çelebi wrote that the foundations were so deep and strong that '…during the initial excavations… they descended so deeply that even the ox which carries the world on his horns heard their noise'.

According to Evliya's account, once the mosque was complete, in order to express how sound the dome was, Sinan told Sultan Suleyman that on Judgment Day, even if the mountains were thrown around like cotton flying in the wind, the mosque's dome might roll like a ball, but would not be destroyed.

The Mosque

THE INNER COURTYARD

The Süleymaniye mosque's forecourt, or *iç avlu*, is a simple rectangle, paved in white marble, sometimes called the 'white harem' – in the sense of protected space. A large rectangular marble fountain, with flat-top (Bursa) arches, stands at the centre. Curiously, it is not equipped with the usual spouts found on an ablution fountain (*şadırvan*). Since Sinan made the innovation of placing taps for ritual washing before prayer under loggias on the east and west façades of the mosque, this elegant fountain is not meant for purification. It serves as an ornamental device, its flowing water providing the court with

an aural and visual richness. French ambassador Philippe du Fresne-Canaye, who saw the fountain in 1573, compared its beauty to the celebrated grottoes of Naples.

The inner courtyard is surrounded on all four sides by an arcade (*revak*) with twenty-eight domes. The portico, the area for latecomers to prayer, or *son cemaat yeri*, is higher than the rest of the arcade. Moreover, the dome directly above the door to the prayer hall is elevated above those flanking it, accentuating the axis that runs through the entrance to the *mihrap* (the niche in the *kıble* wall inside the mosque that indicates the direction of Mecca). Two entrances open to the forecourt where its east and west walls join those of the mosque. A third gate is situated in the courtyard's north wall.

RIGHT
North portal of the forecourt. This monumental entrance is unique in classical Ottoman architecture.

OPPOSITE
Süleymaniye mosque from the southwest, showing part of the outer courtyard and the plaza of Tiryaki Çarşısı.

The monumental form of this north entryway is striking. Aligned on the same axis as the door to the prayer hall and the *mihrap*, the portal is three-stories high, about one third higher than the courtyard walls. This is the first and last time in classical Ottoman architecture that a portal this large was used. Each of its floors was designed as a small apartment. Evliya Çelebi reported that these spaces were assigned to the mosque's personnel: the *bevvab* (gatekeeper), the *muvakkit* (timekeeper, for prayer services) and others.

The arch above the recessed door is ornamented with stalactite-vaulting, *mukarnas* (the main entryway to the prayer hall has a similar vault). Above the arch is a panel inscribed with the Islamic profession of faith: 'There is no god but God, and

Muhammad is the Messenger of God'. The portal is crowned by triangular crests fringed with palmettes. This imposing gate, a unique type in Ottoman architectural history, resembles the entryways of Mamluk *medreses*, though on a smaller scale. During his long career in the military, Sinan served in a number of campaigns in distant lands. Perhaps this atypical entrance was an attempt to reflect in his design what he had observed and experienced in different cultural milieus.

THE MINARETS

Four minarets occupy the corners of the forecourt. (Apparently, Sinan was influenced by the plan of the Üç Şerefeli mosque at Edirne, constructed nearly one hundred years earlier, which had

BELOW
The outer courtyard and the north façade of the forecourt. The 'jewelled minaret' is in the background.

the same pattern.) One pair, each with three balconies, seventy-six metres tall, is located where the east and west walls of the courtyard connect with the north façade of the building. The other pair, each with two balconies, rises fifty-six metres high and stands at the opposite sides of the forecourt. A single row of turquoise tiles adorns each of the minarets directly below their pointed caps. Because of their different heights, the minarets create a powerful sense of depth from various angles. When viewed from the direction of Golden Horn, they elevate the mosque's rather low silhouette extending from the central dome to the end of the inner courtyard.

There is a story, perhaps apocryphal, that when the Safavid ruler of Persia, Shah Tahmasp I (r. 1524–76), heard that Süleyman had temporarily suspended construction of the mosque because of depleted funds, he sent an emissary with a letter to the Ottoman court, along with a quantity of jewels and coin. 'We have been told that your power is insufficient to complete your mosque, so we send an abundant treasury and jewels, to assist,' wrote the shah. 'Spend these and complete the mosque'.

Süleyman was angered by the shah's impudence. He distributed the money to the labourers and gave the jewels to Sinan. 'These stones are worthless compared to my mosque', he declared. 'Add them to the building blocks'. The minaret with three balconies on the left of the inner courtyard (when facing the entrance to the prayer hall) is commonly known as the 'jewelled minaret', because Sinan supposedly mixed the precious stones in its mortar.

THE OUTER COURTYARD

A large outer court (dış avlu) encloses the mosque and forecourt on three sides. The walls of this external precinct are lower than those of the inner courtyard, and they are pierced by windows and doors opening onto the neighbouring streets. Travellers have reported that the court was covered with sand in centuries past. It was also filled with plane trees, clusters of willows,

cypresses, linden trees, elms and ash trees, and the wall on the side overlooking the Golden Horn was deliberately kept low, so as not to disrupt the view.

The cool winds that blow off the Bosphorus make it particularly pleasant here in the summer. Today, as in Evliya Çelebi's time, visitors come to enjoy the dramatic vista, which encompasses a broad sweep of city districts, including Eminönü, Üsküdar, Tophane, Galata, Beyoğlu, Kasımpaşa and even Okmeydanı.

THE PRAYER HALL

The main approach to the Süleymaniye mosque's prayer hall is from the north, through the inner courtyard. Measuring approximately seventy by sixty-one metres around the exterior, the building has a large central dome set on a cubic understructure. The dome, with pendentives, is 26.2 metres in diameter and 49.5 metres high. It rests on four large arches that spring from four piers. The mosque's upper structure (a central dome joined with two half-domes on the north and south sides) is based on a model used in Hagia Sophia; in the original upper construction of the Fatih mosque (destroyed in an earthquake in 1509); and in the Beyazid mosque of 1505. Undoubtedly, Sinan was influenced by the design of these earlier buildings. During restoration in 2009, more than 200 pipes were discovered in the Süleymaniye's central dome, which served to enhance acoustics, as well as lighten the structure.

The two half-domes attached to the central dome, on the north-south axis to the *mihrap*, are bordered by exedrae. Parallel side aisles are each covered with five domes. The domes in the corners and in the middle are 9.9 metres in diameter; the others are each 7.2 metres. Four large columns occupy the space between the great piers on either side of the building. Those separating the main area from the aisles are made of red granite, the others, white marble. They measure 10.2 metres in height, up to the point where their stalactite encrusted capitals connect to the arches. These columns also support the lateral galleries.

BELOW
Exterior view of the mosque's upper structure (southwest). The main arches that support the central dome, as well as the octagonal weight towers flanking them, can be seen clearly.

Sinan intended for the central dome's supporting structure to be discernible from the outside, and load-bearing elements such as the piers, arches and columns are perceptible on the building's exterior. The lateral triple arches and large columns between the piers inside are reflected in the one set of triple and two sets of double windows on the outer east and west façades. The main arches upon which the dome rests are also defined by the fenestration within them. The light that floods through the many windows makes the interior walls seem almost transparent.

At the summit of the step-like progression of domes that ascends the mosque's exterior, small buttresses encircle the drum of the lead-covered central dome, helping support it. Octagonal weight towers topped by scalloped domes flank the main arches. Extensions of the interior piers that carry the arches, these towers counteract the massive dome's tremendous outward thrust.

OPPOSITE
Loggias fill the space between the buttresses on the east façade. The area below is equipped with taps for ablutions.

BELOW
The west aisle of the prayer hall. In times past, travellers could store their valuables in the area enclosed with grilles, below the gallery.

The walls on all four sides of the mosque are reinforced with buttresses, positioned symmetrically on the axes of the piers that carry the main arches and central dome. Those on the north wall are situated completely inside the building, so as not to disrupt the appearance of the entrance façade, while those on the south wall are placed externally, not to detract from the *mihrap*. By filling the space between the protruding buttresses on the east and west sides of the mosque with loggias, Sinan both created functional space and enhanced the aesthetics of the façades, one of which overlooks the court, the other a busy plaza.

The arcades on the sides of the building are an innovation that Mimar Sinan used for the first time in the Süleymaniye mosque. (At the mosque of Şehzade – which Sinan called his apprentice work – he left the east and west façades empty.) A broad wooden eave above the second tier of galleries protects the area below, equipped with taps for ablutions, from rain and sun.

Besides the main door from the courtyard, two additional entryways on either side of the building open to the prayer hall. These doorways were given names such as the *kıble* door, viziers' door and imam's door. The side entries, each of which has a flight of stone steps, were used more frequently than the main door by those entering and leaving the mosque because they were closest to the adjacent streets and commercial areas. The left entrance from the outer court was traditionally used by the commander of the Janissary corps and his troops when they came to the Süleymaniye for the Friday prayer.

Although the Hagia Sophia's structural scheme of a central dome and two half-domes was undoubtedly the model for the plan of the Süleymaniye mosque, the interior of the latter building is much brighter. The shadow-filled spaces of the Hagia Sophia, especially the side aisles, have given way in the Süleymaniye to a place of light. Windows fill the tympana of the great arches that spring from the piers, and the *mihrap* wall is fenestrated from the floor to the dome. A total of 249 windows give the mosque a radiant luminosity.

The stained glass windows with plaster ribs on either side
of the *mihrap* carry the signature of a master glazier named
Ibrahim. Those above are emblazoned with the ninety-nine most
beautiful names of God (*al-asma' al-husna*). The white plaster in
the building, which is largely unadorned on most of the walls
and the piers, enhances the spaciousness and brightness of the
worship area. Moreover, as in many Ottoman mosques, the
ground-level windows of the prayer hall unite the interior with
the outside. When the shutters are open in summer, the fragrance
of the flowers in the court, as well as light, floods the interior.

In contrast to the high galleries that form a 'U' in the Hagia
Sophia, the lateral galleries in the Süleymaniye mosque are
lower, allowing more light into the worship space at ground
level. Evliya Çelebi reported that sections of the arcade screened
with iron grilles (*maksures*), below the gallery on the west side,
were used as a kind of vault, where travellers could leave money
and valuables.

Prayer hall of the Süleymaniye mosque, looking towards the *mihrap* wall.

The mosque's principal fixtures – the *mihrap*, *minber* (the tall covered dais from which the imam delivers an address during the Friday prayer), sultan's loge and tribune for the muezzins (the givers of the call to prayer) – all display exquisite workmanship and carefully detailed proportions. Blending in with the architecture, they do not interrupt the grand openness of the interior.

The sultan's loge (*hünkâr mahfili*), where the ruler and his entourage prayed separately from the rest of those assembled for prayer, is to the left (east) of the *mihrap*. Consisting of a platform encircled by a railing, atop eight elegant marble columns with pointed arches, it is reached by a staircase inside the wall, which starts in a window. The sultan could enter and depart unobserved through the door from the outer court. The *hünkâr mahfili* has its own small *mihrap*, adorned with stalactites.

The sultan used this loge for Friday prayers, as well as those on religious holidays and Islamic holy nights. On such occasions, the ruler would march in state from the palace to the mosque with a cortege of officials and military units. These ceremonial processions were known as the Friday and holiday parades. The viziers and the commander of the Janissaries, who had arrived at the mosque earlier, would receive the sultan. The Janissary chief first removed the sultan's boots and then, together with the sultan's sword bearer, would offer the ruler his arm and escort him to the loge.

A tribune for the muezzins abuts the pier to the right of the *mihrap*. Fashioned from marble, it is supported by sixteen plain columns. During communal prayers, a muezzin on the platform repeated the *takbir* (the pronouncement 'God is (the) greatest' – '*Allahu akbar*'), uttered at intervals by the imam leading the prayer in front of the *mihrap*, to ensure that it was heard by all the worshippers assembled in the mosque's vast space.

A podium for an imam, on seven columns, is situated at a corner of the opposite pier. Another fixture for an imam, a *kürsü*, or raised seat made of ebony, is supposed to have earned Mimar Sinan's praises for its craftsmanship. The mosque's large wooden doors and window shutters, with their original mother of pearl and tortoiseshell inlay, also display superb workmanship.

Sinan had used coloured stone to decorate the Şehzade mosque both inside and out. He also embellished the minarets with motifs in stone relief and the domes with palmettes to enliven the exterior. By contrast, the Süleymaniye mosque presents a subdued, monochromatic façade. There is more colour in the interior, most strikingly, perhaps, in the alternating red and white voussoirs of the main arches.

A small room above the (north) entrance door of the Süleymaniye mosque is noteworthy. When the window shutters

ABOVE
A *kürsü*, or seat for an imam, fashioned from ebony.

around the prayer hall were closed against the cold, on winter days, the air inside would eventually became polluted by smoke from the hundreds of oil lamps that illuminated the interior, as well as the breath of the worshippers. So Sinan devised a unique ventilation system that channelled the warm, stuffy air into the room above the entryway and thence to the outside. Reportedly, the soot that accumulated on the ceiling of this room was used to make ink of the highest quality.

DECORATION

The most skilled craftsmen and artisans were employed in constructing the Süleymaniye mosque. Even though they used

RIGHT
The muezzins' tribune, adjacent to the southwest pier.

costly materials, ornamentation was consciously restrained both inside and outside of the building. The mosque's endowment deed stresses that it should not be overly embellished, in accordance with the traditions of the Prophet Muhammad. Moreover, in his later years, Sultan Süleyman became much more devout, and he avoided ostentation in his dress and private life. His aversion to luxury is reflected in the decoration of his mosque. He appears to have preferred a measured decoration that did not overwhelm the architectural expression.

The tiles that adorn the Süleymaniye mosque, as well as its mausoleums, were made in Iznik, once the Ottoman capital. Tiles produced there by the technique of underglaze painting had supplanted in popularity the *cuerda seca* tiles (a type of Persian origin), common in earlier Ottoman buildings. By the middle of the sixteenth century, the Iznik kilns were fabricating tiles of the finest quality. The Ottoman palace and those connected with it were the leading purchasers of the tiles, and Sinan used them in important structures.

Iznik tiles were sent to all parts of the empire – to the monasteries of Mount Athos (in present-day Greece), Cairo, Damascus and Jerusalem. One of their most distinctive features was their coral red colour, which remained in light relief on the surface (discernible by touch) from the pigment applied under the glaze. Tiles at the Süleymaniye are among the first to display it. The production technique was employed continually for nearly fifty years, with the formula for the colour passed by word of mouth from master to apprentice until it was eventually forgotten.

Another characteristic of the Iznik tiles is their semi-stylised designs, which replaced the geometric and abstract floral patterns of previous periods. The most frequently repeated motifs are roses, tulips, hyacinths, grape vines, trees with blossoms, cypresses and sometimes apple trees.

Though used sparingly in the Süleymaniye mosque, tiles were ordered for the building by imperial decree in 1552. Then as now, they were expensive items. Süleyman's reign was the

BELOW
Calligraphic medallion rendered in tiles, next to the *mihrap*, which displays verses from Surat al-Fatihah, the first chapter of the Qur'an.

richest period of the Ottoman Empire, and the ruler could have covered the interior of the mosque with them had he wished. Yet, only the *mihrap* wall inside the building, and the area above the windows of the portico on the exterior are decorated with tiles. It would seem that the sultan and his architect agreed on a minimal degree of adornment.

The wall around the *mihrap* is bordered in tiles with white Chinese cloud motifs on a turquoise background. However, perhaps the most impressive tile decorations in the mosque are the round medallions, 210 centimetres in diameter, on either side of the *mihrap*. They display verses of Surat al-Fatihah (The Opening), the first chapter of the Qur'an, in large *sülüs* calligraphy (Ar. *thuluth*, a cursive style of Arabic script often used in mosque decoration), which emerge from a geometric pattern in the centre. (Verses 1–4 are on the right, and 5–7 on the left.)

Restoration done on the north face of the two piers near the *mihrap* in 2010 revealed traces of sixteenth-century tiled inscriptions. They were discovered beneath writing done on wood by the famous nineteenth-century calligrapher Abdulfettah Efendi (*d.* 1896). The blue, turquoise, green, and white panels essentially repeat the form and content of the round medallions on either sides of the *mihrap*.

Calligraphy is at the fore in the decoration of the Süleymaniye mosque. Most of the inscriptions are the work of Hasan bin Ahmed el-Karahisari, who was the adopted son and student of

ABOVE
Qur'anic passages adorn the windows in the forecourt.

OVERLEAF
Illuminated by a band of windows at the base, the central dome displays Qur'an 35:41, which begins, 'Lo! Allah graspeth the heavens and the earth . . .'.

Ahmed el-Karahisari (*d.* 1556), regarded as one of the greatest calligraphers of the period. Accounting records for the mosque's construction reveal information about his wages, materials and methods. For instance, to produce the calligraphic tile panels, he first wrote the texts on paper rolls in Istanbul and then sent them to Iznik to be copied onto the tiles and fired.

The most exemplary calligraphy is in the inner courtyard over the doors and windows, inside the central dome, within the pendentives, between the arches and on panels hanging from the walls. Even if much of the populace could not read the Arabic writing, the inscriptions were esteemed as passages from the Holy Qur'an and appreciated for their exquisite artistry.

Rectangular tile lunettes, displaying white *sülüs* calligraphy on a blue field, adorn the tops of the windows on the mosque's north façade, in the forecourt. *Ayat al-kursi*, 'the Throne Verse' (number 255 of the Qur'an's Surat al-Baqarah, Chapter of the Cow), which avows the absolute sovereignty of the all-knowing God, appears to the right of the main door, and the twenty-ninth verse of the Victory Chapter (Surat al-Fath) is on the left, which promises God's 'forgiveness and immense reward' to those followers of His Messenger (Muhammad) who bow and prostrate themselves in worship, seeking bounty and acceptance from God.

A tripartite inscription on marble panels in the mosque's stalactite encrusted entryway includes titles of honour for Sultan Süleyman: 'the shadow of God over all peoples', 'the conqueror of lands of the East and West', and 'the sultan of the sultans of the Persians and the Arabs'. Here one learns at a glance that the ruler presided over a domain of universal dimensions. Ebussuud Efendi, the *şeyhülislam* (chief religious authority in the Ottoman state), designated the contents of the inscriptions. Many texts compare the mosque to paradise, or summon believers to prayer – especially the Friday prayer – with passages from the Qur'an. The religious views of the state determined jointly by the sultan and Ebussuud (namely, institutionalised Sunni theology) are clearly reflected in the inscriptions.

The text at the mosque's main entrance that stresses Süleyman's supremacy over the Persians was undoubtedly influenced by contemporary events. While the building was being erected, the Ottomans twice set off on campaign against the Shi'i Safavids of Persia. The first expedition ended without achieving its aim, and the Ottoman army was unable to realise a decisive victory in the second. Nevertheless, the peace treaty of Amasya (29 May 1555) provided the Ottomans with important political gains. Among them, the Safavid ruler, Shah Tahmasp I, agreed to cease trying to further his influence and Shi'i belief in Ottoman territory, demonstrating respect for the Ottomans' adherence to Sunni doctrine, which is strongly emphasised in the inscriptions of the Süleymaniye mosque.

Some chroniclers have identified Sultan Süleyman with another religious and historical figure – the Prophet Süleyman in the Qur'an (Solomon of the Bible). In the endowment deed for the Süleymaniye, the sultan is recognised as the Süleyman of the age, that is, Süleyman the prophet of the time. Even Shah Tahmasp, the sultan's rival, compared him to the eminent Süleyman of the past, in terms of justice, wisdom and riches.

The Ottomans developed an order of placement for inscriptions in their mosques (somewhat akin to the hierarchical positioning of icons in orthodox Christian churches). Accordingly, the word for God, the name of the Prophet, the names of the first four caliphs (or successors of the Prophet), and verses from the Qur'an are situated in specific areas of the Süleymaniye mosque.

In the pendentives above the *mihrap*, 'Allah' is written on the right and 'Muhammad' on the left in large roundels. The circular panels at the top of the

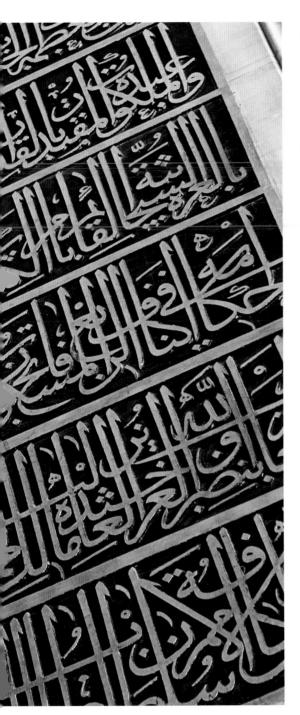

main piers contain the names of the first four caliphs of Islam (Abu Bakr, 'Umar, 'Uthman, and 'Ali), while those in the pendentives over the north entry door exhibit the names of the Prophet Muhammad's grandsons, Hassan and Husayn. Verse seventy-nine of the sixth chapter of the Qur'an (Surat al-An'am, Chapter of the Cattle) appears in the half-dome above the *mihrap*, and the forty-first verse of Surat al-Fatir (The Creator) is displayed in the central dome – 'Lo! Allah graspeth the heavens and the earth that they deviate not, and if they were to deviate there is not one that could grasp them after Him. Lo! He is ever Clement, Forgiving'.

While renovating the dome in 2009–10, restorers discovered that the writing was painted on sheet metal rather than plaster. The calligrapher Abdulfettah Efendi completed this work during restorations in the 1850s, in the reign of Sultan Abdulmecid (1837–61).

Construction of the Süleymaniye

The Turkish historian Ömer Lutfi Barkan has uncovered a wealth of information in the account books for the construction of the Süleymaniye. These records identify the workers, as well as the building materials, their origin, and where they were used. They also describe daily events. Materials from the four corners of the Ottoman Empire came to the mosque's construction site. Columns and huge pieces of marble were brought from the cities of antiquity. Sometimes ancient city walls had to be knocked down in order to remove them, and special ships built to transport them.

The French scholar Pierre Gilles (1490–1555), who lived in Istanbul between 1549 and 1551, witnessed the removal of seventeen marble columns from the old Byzantine hippodrome (today's Sultanahmet Square). Another sixteenth-century European visitor to the city, Hans Dernschwan, records that marble steps were taken from the same site. He also mentions

that material was salvaged from the ruins of ancient Nicomedia (present-day Izmit).

Imperial decrees indicate that priceless columns and stones were collected from Baalbek (in today's Lebanon), ancient monuments in Mut, Silifke and Alanya, and various cities of antiquity in Anatolia and the Balkan Peninsula. Reportedly, two of the four huge red columns (9.1 metres in height and 1.26 in diameter) that carry the lateral arches between the piers of the central dome came from Alexandria and Baalbek respectively. Istanbul is the supposed provenance of the other two. One was apparently found at Topkapı Palace, and the second, dating

from the Roman era, was transferred to the construction site in
1551 from its original location in the vicinity of the Column of
Marcian, in the present-day district of Fatih.

Tezkiretü'l-bünyan (a brief biography of Sinan and a list of his
buildings by the poet-painter Mustafa Sai Çelebi, *d.* 1595–6)
describes how this column was transported and put in place.
By order of the sultan, the main masts of galleons were used to
construct huge scaffolding. Enormous wheels were turned from
the inside by soldiers, and big pulleys and hawsers as thick as
a human body were used to raise the colossal column from its
place and put it on sledges to be moved to the building site.

The construction records also show that round porphyry stone was removed from the Orhan Bey *medrese* in Iznik and transported to the Süleymaniye mosque. Wood was brought from the Black Sea shores near Istanbul and from Biga, south of the Marmara; brick from Istanbul's Hasköy and from Gelibolu; iron from Bulgaria; hawsers and ropes from around Samsun; and mortar and lime from the environs of Istanbul, Bursa and Izmit.

The Divan-ı Hümayun (Imperial Council) summoned craftsmen and artisans – Muslim and Christian alike – from the four corners of the Ottoman Empire to work on the Süleymaniye. Conscripts and slaves provided the unskilled

labour. The largest groups of craftsmen were the brick layers and stonecutters, followed by the carpenters, blacksmiths, painters, glaziers, tinsmiths and sappers. According to the season, the number of workers ranged between 2,000 and 3,000, rising during the summer and spring months but falling in the winter, when work sometimes stopped completely.

During the seven years of construction, ceremonies were held to mark certain milestones and awards were given to the workers. For instance, gifts were distributed when the building rose above foundation level, when the big arches that carried the dome were raised and when the dome was closed.

Evliya Çelebi probably exaggerates when he declares that each of the four colossal red columns between the main piers was worth ten times the entire treasury of Egypt. The chronicler Ibrahim Peçevi (1572–1650) reports that 896,380 florins and 82,900 silver pieces were spent to complete the complex. Yet, the total cost of construction is impossible to calculate exactly.

ABOVE
The huge columns between the piers in the prayer hall were reused from ancient monuments in Istanbul, Alexandria and Baalbek.

Once erected, the Süleymaniye's operational expenses, such as providing food for the 700 people who worked in the complex, were immense. The cost of administration, upkeep, and repair was met from the *vakıf*, or pious foundation, established by the sultan to support the Süleymaniye. A number of sources generated the income, including 221 villages, 30 arable fields, seven mills, two weirs for fishing, two wharves, one pasture, two farms, two islands, two city districts and the output of five hamlets.

The relationship between Sultan Süleyman and his architect during the construction of the Süleymaniye was at times tense, as recounted in Mustafa Sai Çelebi's biography of Mimar Sinan. Sinan was involved in other projects during the building of the Süleymaniye, and at one point, when the sultan was residing at Edirne, jealous rivals apparently notified the ruler about his additional work. Sinan was also accused of becoming so enamoured with making the huge central dome that it consumed him, and he neglected his overall task.

One day, while Sinan was talking with the stonemasons about how to cut the *mihrap* and *minber*, the sultan arrived at the construction site unexpectedly. Angrily, he asked why the architect was occupied with other people's work and ignoring his own. He also demanded to know when the mosque would be finished. Surprised by this challenge, Sinan responded that it would be completed in two months. After returning to Topkapı Palace with his entourage, the sultan exclaimed: 'The chief architect has gone mad. The work cannot be finished in a year, let alone two months! He has lost his mind out of fear. Send for him at once and question him'.

Sinan remained calm. He went to the palace and reiterated that he would finish the building in two months. Then he apparently summoned all the artisans and expert craftsmen in Istanbul and, working night and day, finished the work by the promised date.

When the writers of the period discuss the Süleymaniye, they always reserve the greatest praise for the mosque. Numerous sources identify it with the personality of Süleyman. Nonetheless, all buildings of the Süleymaniye together provide compelling evidence of the ruler's persona and the Ottoman presence in Istanbul.

Various chroniclers assert that the ten balconies on the mosque's minarets symbolised Süleyman's being the tenth

Ottoman sultan. The same imagery appears in the building's foundation registers. The Ottoman historian Celalzade, Mustafa Çelebi (*c.* 1490–1567), however, claimed that the number of balconies signified the ten companions of the Prophet Muhammad to whom paradise was promised (*al-'asharah al-mubashsharah*). Moreover, both Mustafa Sai Çelebi and Celalzade likened the mosque's dome to the Prophet, as the protector of the religion of Islam. Besides this comparison, the building's minarets were identified with the first four caliphs. Mustafa Sai Çelebi also stated that the mosque was akin to the Ka'aba at Mecca and the four piers that carried the dome represented the four caliphs.

The Mausoleums

SULTAN SÜLEYMAN'S TOMB

Beginning with Mehmed the Conqueror, Ottoman rulers adopted the custom of constructing their mausoleums behind the *kıble* wall of their memorial mosques. Sultan Süleyman's tomb was also erected in this tradition, on the same axis as the Süleymaniye mosque's *mihrap* and main entrances to the inner courtyard and prayer hall.

Süleyman was 71 years old when he died (7 September 1566) while on campaign in Hungary, and his body was temporarily interred under the throne in his tent. Following the victory of the Ottoman army, the sultan's coffin was first brought to Belgrade by horse carriage, where it was met ceremoniously by his son, Selim II (*r.* 1566–74), and then transported to Istanbul. There it was carried to the cemetery of the Süleymaniye mosque in solemn procession. The *Tarih-i Sultan Süleyman* (The History of Sultan Süleyman), by the Ottoman historiographer Seyyid Lokman (*fl. c.* 1569–96), illustrates this event in a miniature painting.

The leading members of the state are portrayed in mourning attire, carrying the sultan's coffin on their shoulders. Süleyman's crested turban is tied to the coffin, and an officer walks in

OPPOSITE
A miniature from Lokman's *Tarih-i Sultan Süleyman* portrays a procession of mourners carrying Süleyman's coffin, while others dig his grave in the cemetery behind his mosque. The depictions of Hürrem Sultan's tomb and the residence of the cemetery caretaker (right) are the earliest pictorial representations of these buildings.

front, carrying a golden casket above his head. This might have contained the sultan's inner organs, but probably held personal effects to be placed in his tomb. Süleyman's freshly dug grave is visible behind the courtyard wall. A white-bearded figure holding a wooden cubit rod is thought to be Mimar Sinan, and a temporary tent covering the gravesite marks the spot where he would erect the sultan's mausoleum.

Surrounded by an ambulatory and an arcade that joins a portico with five bays at the entrance, the sultan's octagonal mausoleum is reminiscent of late Roman funerary monuments. On all sides, windows are set in the tympana of the arches on the high drum of the exterior dome. An inner dome (the top of which reaches the cornice of the upper eave adorned with palmettes) is fully buried in the drum. This second dome rests on an elegant arcade that encircles the interior of the tomb.

The mausoleum was erected by Süleyman's successor, Selim II, but the sultan had undoubtedly specified its architectural and decorative scheme before his death. The building resembles the Dome of the Rock in Jerusalem, the oldest and best-known structure in Islamic architecture; yet, there are significant points of difference. For instance, Suleyman's tomb has a much more modest exterior.

Although the outside of the structure is restrained, the interior is richly embellished. Two tile panels with motifs of budding flowers adorn either side of the mausoleum's entry door. A piece of the black stone from the Ka'aba embedded in the keystone of the arch over the entrance enhances the sanctity of the sepulchre. Inside, eight precious columns (four pink and four white), supporting the richly decorated dome, surround the coffins in the middle. Sunburst motifs (fashioned by incising the plaster with the point of a trowel) spread out radially from the centre of the dome. Rock crystals implanted in these designs shine in the low light that streams through the windows. The use of semi-precious stones reflects a Persian tradition that is not frequently found in Ottoman decoration.

Tile roundels in the pendentives beneath the dome display the word Allah and the names Muhammed (the Prophet); Abu Bakr, 'Umar, 'Uthman, and 'Ali (the first four caliphs); and Hassan and Husayn (the Prophet's grandsons). Underneath the windows, what appears to be a band of alternating coloured marble panels is actually painted stucco. Below this, *Ayat al-kursi* and other verses from Surat al-Baqarah are emblazoned in white *sülüs* script on the band of blue tiles. Inscriptions containing eight of the most beautiful names of God are embossed on the stalactite capitals of the columns: Ya Muhyi ('O Giver of Life'), Ya Mumit ('O Taker of Life'), Ya Qawi ('O Possessor of All Strength'), Ya Sami' ('O All-Hearing'), Ya Basir ('O All-Seeing'), Ya 'Alim ('O All-Knowing'), Ya Khaliq ('O Creator'), Ya Razzaq ('O Sustainer').

The mausoleum contains seven sarcophagi, of which the largest, with a turban, belongs to Sultan Süleyman. The other two with turbans, to the left, are those of Sultans Süleyman II (*r.* 1687–91) and Ahmed II (*r.* 1691–5). The rest of the coffins belong to Süleyman's favourite daughter, Mihrimah (*d.* 1578), and other female members of the Ottoman family.

Sixteenth-century European visitors to the mausoleum recounted that the sultan's bow and arrows were displayed there, symbolic of his status as a *gazi*, or victorious fighter for the Islamic faith. Apparently, a white turban with a black crested pendant and a caftan that Süleyman wore on his final campaign were also on exhibit, along with models of the holy buildings he had repaired in Mecca and Medina during his reign. An official cadre of those who had memorised the Qur'an recited it continuously, and freshly cut flowers in porcelain vases gave the tomb a lovely odour.

HÜRREM SULTAN'S TOMB

The second mausoleum behind the Süleymaniye mosque's *kıble* wall is that of Süleyman's wife, Haseki Hürrem Sultan (*d.* 1558) – known to the West as Roxelana, the Russian. Born Aleksandra Lisowska, she was a concubine of Polish origin from Rohatyn in present-day Ukraine. After entering the palace, she was given the name Hürrem, which means 'smiling' and 'joyful' in Persian. She and Süleyman experienced a love that was unparalleled in the history of the Ottoman dynasty, and their marriage lasted forty years. Historical sources relate that she won the sultan's heart not with her beauty but with her gaiety, likeableness, sweet tongue and elegance. The depth of their love is evidenced in the letters that they exchanged during Süleyman's long campaigns.

Never before had an Ottoman ruler married a concubine and raised her to the status of wedded wife. Moreover, neither before nor after Süleyman's reign were double mausoleums constructed for a sultan and his wife. Hürrem Sultan was recognised as a monarch both in the East and the West, and she established diplomatic relations with foreign courts. In the letters from the Polish ruler King Sigismund, he addressed her as 'my fellow countrywoman'. Among the gifts that Shah Tahmasp sent to the

Ottoman capital upon the completion of the Süleymaniye mosque were presents from the Shah's wife to Hürrem Sultan, accompanied by a letter filled with adulation.

Sinan designed the interior of Hürrem Sultan's mausoleum to resemble a vision of the gardens of paradise. The entrance to the domed, octagonal structure is through a portico with three bays. Qur'anic verses, including *Ayat al-kursi*, are carved in relief in monumental *sülüs* script on the exterior of the dome's drum. The interior is adorned with blue-ground tiles displaying blossoming branches, tulips, and carnations. The alternating windows and stalactite niches in the sepulchre are also covered with a rich assortment of tiles.

Sunburst motifs, dagger-like leaves, budding branches, palmettes, tulips and various stylised vegetal designs truly suggest an image of the Garden of Eden and the dome of paradise, with which the Süleymaniye's endowment deed compares the tomb. European travellers relate that vases of flowers once filled the mausoleum, and that Hürrem Sultan's coffin was draped with a covering of costly material and mounted with a headdress and priceless jewelled brooch.

At the rear of the funerary garden, behind the mausoleums of Süleyman and Hürrem Sultan, and flush with the courtyard wall, is a square, domed structure known as the *türbedar odası* (mausoleum caretaker's building). It also served as a *darülkurra*, or Qur'an readers' room.

The Schools and Other Buildings

The four principal schools of the Süleymaniye were built approximately a century after those at the Fatih complex (called the 'eight courtyards'). They represented the pinnacle of Ottoman educational institutions. Known as the first, second, third, and fourth *medreses*, they were built, as mentioned by Evliya Çelebi, for the four schools of law in Sunni Islam: Hanafi, Hanbali, Maliki, and Shafi'i. They were situated, two each, on the east and west sides of the Süleymaniye mosque.

Lessons were given five days a week in the *medreses*, with Tuesdays and Fridays as holidays. Islamic law and theology served as the basis of the curriculum, as well as Qur'anic interpretation (*tefsir*) and traditions (*hadis*). Besides these customary branches of learning, training was provided in subjects such as mathematics and geometry. Graduates of the *medreses* could work in the legal, judicial and educational fields. If they chose to enter the bureaucracy, they could reach the

highest ranks, such as *şeyhülislam* or *kazasker* (chief judicial authority in the Ottoman state).

The basic *medrese* design consists of rooms arranged in a 'U' or 'L' pattern around a courtyard with arcades. The rooms, or cells, were spartan, usually consisting of a bed and a fireplace for one tutor or two students. This model had existed since the Middle Ages, and Mimar Sinan did not alter it, except for introducing a few notable innovations in plan.

The first and second schools, face the plaza of Tiryaki Çarşısı, near a large public fountain, known as Çadır Çeşmesi, or the Tent Fountain, because of its shape. They are built symmetrically on either side of a narrow alley. These *medreses*, which are at the highest level of the *külliye* topographically, each contain twenty-three cells and one classroom, as well as quarters for the teacher and toilets. The teachers' housing is an originality that Sinan brought to *medrese* architecture.

A primary school with two sections is located next to the first *medrese*. The closed portion served as a dormitory, and the

BELOW
Tiryaki Çarşısı, view to the south.
The Süleymaniye's medical
school is on the right, and the
wall of the mosque's outer court
is on the left.

OPPOSITE
The hospice of the Süleymaniye
complex (background), seen from
a minaret.

open area functioned as a classroom. Spacious houses were also built for the teachers in the near vicinity, and space for stores was made in the lower façades of the schools, fronting the plaza, to generate income for the Süleymaniye complex. Today, the *medreses* house a library with one of the richest manuscript collections of the Islamic world. It includes numerous volumes embellished with gilding, miniatures, exquisite calligraphy and the art of *ebru* (paper marbling). Handwritten copies of all of the works of the renowned Islamic scholar Ibn Sina (known in the West as Avicenna, *d.* 1037), some of which date from the eleventh century CE, are in the Süleymaniye Library.

A medical school was eventually erected next to the second *medrese*, at the order of the sultan. Its original architecture was altered when it was later converted into a childbirth clinic. The medical students looked after the patients in a hospital, which was also part of the complex, opposite the school to the north.

The hospital accommodated 40–50 beds, and its charter specified that medicine should be prepared on its premises. Those on duty included three doctors, two eye specialists, two surgeons and one pharmacist. Polyclinic diagnosis was undertaken, and in a section for patients with mental illnesses, music was among the treatments used. The hospital's large pharmaceutical depot, the *darül'akakir*, provided other Istanbul hospitals with medicine. A *hamam* in the northwest corner was reserved for patients, and there was an oven for cooking their meals. This facility continued to serve as a hospital up to the end of the nineteenth century.

The soup kitchen flanking the hospital to the east consisted of a kitchen and dining hall. The hall had five domes, and a separate entrance from the street. The carefully prepared food was noted for being especially appetizing. (Meals were even cooked here for Mimar Sinan, who resided nearby.) Today this building functions as a restaurant.

A hospice was built to the west of the soup kitchen. This building, as well as the kitchen, could only be constructed by terracing the slope on which it lies and supporting it with a

substructure. The lower space was used for a caravanserai, in addition to 'bachelor rooms', which housed poor men who came from Anatolia looking for work.

The third and fourth *medreses* on the east side of the mosque, overlooking the Golden Horn, also lie on a steep grade. They comprise twenty-one rooms in a 'U' shape that descend the slope in step-like fashion, neither blocking the view from the mosque, nor, when seen from the water, distorting the grandeur of the building's profile from the dome to ground level.

Southeast of the mosque's outer courtyard is a school of *hadis*. Its rooms form an 'L' shape and face the Sea of Marmara. The stairs descending from the school lead to the street below, lined with shops.

The building farthest from the complex is the men's *hamam*. Compared to the other buildings in the Süleymaniye complex, this public bath is simple, comprising a single-domed cooling room, a rectangular warm room, four hot rooms, and connected bathing cubicles. It is known as the Dökmeciler (Metal Workers) Hamam, after an adjacent market for metalware.

Mimar Sinan

Little information exists about architects in Ottoman historical sources, and there are no extant texts that describe their conceptual theories and construction techniques. Unlike their European contemporaries, Ottoman builders apparently did not record their understanding of architecture, or of

mathematics, geometry, engineering, and construction materials. No book exists that provides both theoretical and practical information on Ottoman architecture, similar to *De re aedificatoria* (On the Art of Building) by Leon Battista Alberti (1404–72) or *I quattro libri dell'architectura* (The Four Books on Architecture) by Andrea Palladio (1508–80). Ottoman architects – who developed an entirely original design for domed structures – seem to have transmitted knowledge orally from generation to generation. Yet, they drew plans and constructed models, as revealed by documentary and visual evidence. For instance, a contemporary miniature by the painter Nakkaş Osman, in *Surname-i hümayun* (The Book of Imperial Festivities), portrays a model of the Süleymaniye mosque being carried on a large palanquin.

Ottoman buildings that are part of pious foundations, such as the Süleymaniye, are remembered by the names of their patrons, while those who designed them remain anonymous. Even though Sinan served the state for fifty years and built every type of structure from mosques to schools and fountains to mausoleums, he only put his signature on a single bridge at Büyükçekmece, near Istanbul. *Tezkiretü'l-bünyan*, a biography of Sinan in verse, by his contemporary and friend, Mustafa Sai Çelebi, is regarded by scholars as the most trustworthy source about the architect's life and achievements. Other biographies include *Tuhfetü'l-mimarin* and *Tezkiretü'l-ebniye*. These books list the buildings – from viaducts to mausoleums – for which Sinan was responsible.

Mustafa Sai Celebi's treatise and various foundation registers reveal that Sinan became a Janissary after being recruited through the *devşirme* in the province of Kayseri in Cappadocia. The *devşirme*, or periodic levy of young boys, relied on collecting several thousand children from rural villages in the Balkans, Anatolia and the Caucasus and educating them to serve the sultan. They were primarily Christian youth between nine and fifteen years old. Jews and urban children were excluded. The *devşirme* occurred every few years, and the most intelligent and handsome boys would study in the palace school to serve in the court. According to their talents, they could rise to important positions within the state bureaucracy.

The *devşirme* reached Sinan's village of Agirnas (predominantly inhabited by Greeks), in Kayseri province, during the reign of Selim I (1512–20). Sinan probably entered into imperial service at this time. A contemporary treatise on architecture, *Risale-i mimariye*, mentions him as Sinan of Kayseri, alluding to his background. A letter he wrote years later to Sultan Selim II, when he was chief architect, offers further evidence about his specific origins. The letter requests that his relatives from Agirnas not be deported to repopulate the island of Cyprus, which the sultan had conquered in 1572.

Sinan's name appears in different forms in various sources. For example, in *Tezkiretü'l-bünyan* and *Tezkiretü'l-ebniye* he is called Sinan son of Abdulmemnan, and in one of his foundation registers it is Sinan Ağa son of Abdurrahman. On the bridge at Büyükçekmece, he wrote the phrase, 'The work of Yusuf, son of Abdullah'. These names underscore that Sinan was recruited in the *devşirme*. Boys taken in the levy generally adopted Muslim patronymics like Abdullah (Servant of God) or Abdurrahman (Servant of the Compassionate) in place of their fathers' names.

Sinan began to serve as a Janissary in the Ottoman army in 1521. He took part in attacks on Rhodes and Belgrade; the battle of Mohács (1526); and campaigns in Central Europe and against the Safavids of Persia. Trained as a carpenter, he constructed a ship on Lake Van in 1533, during the war with the Safavids. In 1538, while fighting in the Moldavian campaign, he erected a bridge over the Pruth River, which demonstrated his skills as an engineer and builder.

A major turning point in Sinan's career occurred when the newly appointed grand vizier Lutfi Pasha (*d.* 1562–3) offered him the chance to build a mausoleum for his predecessor, Ayas Pasha, in 1539. In the same year, Sinan was appointed Reis-i Mimaran-ı Dergah-ı Ali, or Chief Architect of the Exalted Porte (the Ottoman government), a position he held for forty years, under three different sultans. By the time of his death in 1588, he had completed nearly 500 building and restoration projects in Ottoman territory on three continents. About 300 were in Istanbul and its environs. With the exception of the Selimiye mosque and complex in Edirne, his most original architectural achievements were in the Ottoman capital.

During his youth and service as a Janissary, Sinan was exposed to various cultures in different lands. In Anatolia he saw examples of ancient Greek and Roman, Byzantine, Armenian and Seljuk architecture; in Iran and Iraq, Great Seljuk and Mongol edifices; in Central Europe, structures of the European Middle Ages and Renaissance; and in Rhodes, the Gothic architecture characteristic of the Crusaders. His later works reflect elements from these diverse architectural styles.

Little is known about Sinan's personal life, but deeds from his foundations show that he acquired significant property

OPPOSITE
The tomb of Mimar Sinan. The central dome of the Süleymaniye mosque is visible in the background.

during his career, including 23 houses; 34 shops; a mill, vegetable garden, and boathouse; two inns; five fountains; three schools and one small mosque. His wives were Gülruh and Mihri, and he had five daughters and two sons.

Sinan's tomb was erected on a triangular plot of land just outside the walls of the Süleymaniye complex. It was adjacent to the house of his later years, as well as a school that he had founded. The headquarters of the Janissaries (where the office of the Mufti of Istanbul is now located) was also nearby.

Sinan designed a modest tomb for himself, surrounded by arches on four sides and covered with a dome. The headstone is crowned with a turban. The site also has a domed public

OPPOSITE
The inscription on Mimar Sinan's tomb entreats those who pass to pray for the soul of the departed and recite the Fatihah.

fountain. Over the prayer window in front of the tomb, there is an epitaph by his friend Mustafa Sai Çelebi that contains a chronogram, from which one can deduce the date. The calligraphy was produced by Hasan bin Ahmed el-Karahisari, who had provided the inscriptions for the Süleymaniye mosque. In part, it reads:

> O you, who settle for a day or two in life's palace,
> The world is not a place of repose for man.
>
> Becoming the architect of Süleyman Khan, this
> distinguished man
> Built him a Friday mosque that is a sign of the highest
> paradise...
>
> Sai the well-wisher said the date of his departure:
> 'Passed away from the world at this time, Sinan,
> The patron saint of architects, 996 [1587/88]'
> May old and young offer the Fatihah for his soul.*

Accordingly, Sinan must have been around 100 years old when he died. *Risale-i mimariye* states that he passed away when he was 107, and Evliya Çelebi claims he was 170 years old — a forgivable exaggeration to accentuate the legendary status of this great architect.

*Extracted from the translation of the epitaph in Gülru Necipoğlu, *The Age of Sinan*, London 2011, p. 147.

Today

Despite having lost many of its original functions, the Süleymaniye remains one of Istanbul's important hubs. The schools that once provided various types and levels of education are now a magnet for researchers who come both to view the places where Ottoman religious scholars were educated and to research the treasury of their written works held in the Süleymaniye Library. The *darüzziyafe* soup kitchen has become a popular restaurant, under the same name, which is famous for its Ottoman cuisine. Shops located on every side of the complex zealously continue their centuries-old trades. Although many have been destroyed by fires and negligence, some of the old houses in which teachers and religious authorities lived until the past century greet us on the surrounding streets, where the special fabric of sixteenth-century Istanbul continues to exist.

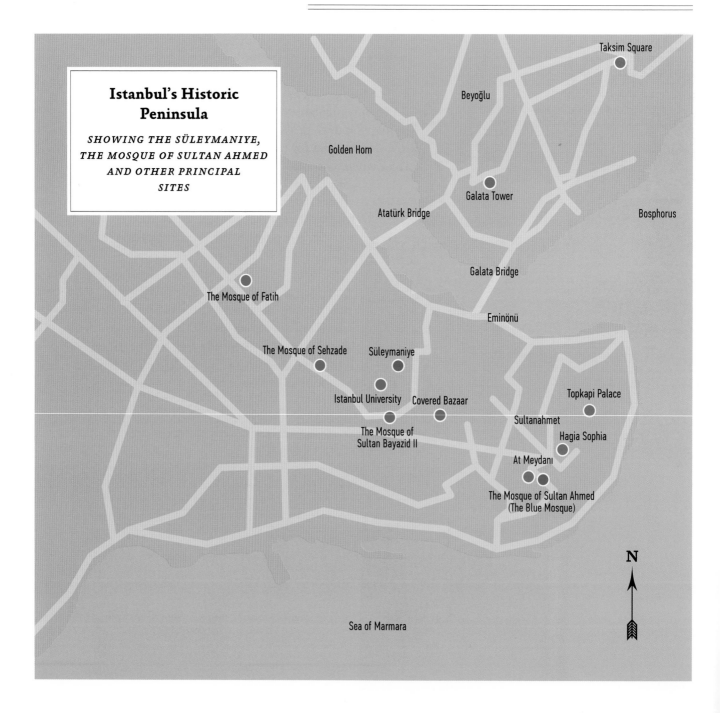

Istanbul's Historic
Peninsula

*SHOWING THE SÜLEYMANIYE,
THE MOSQUE OF SULTAN AHMED
AND OTHER PRINCIPAL
SITES*

Taksim Square

Beyoğlu

Golden Horn

Galata Tower

Atatürk Bridge

Bosphorus

Galata Bridge

Eminönü

The Mosque of Fatih

The Mosque of Sehzade   Süleymaniye

Istanbul University   Covered Bazaar   Topkapi Palace

The Mosque of
Sultan Bayazid II   Sultanahmet

Hagia Sophia

At Meydanı

The Mosque of Sultan Ahmed
(The Blue Mosque)

N

Sea of Marmara

The Istanbul Peninsula, *c.* 1920

This unique photograph, one of the earliest images of Istanbul captured from the air, shows the broad sweep of the city's centre from ancient through Ottoman times and almost all of the principal monuments erected there over the centuries, including the Süleymaniye and the mosque and complex of Sultan Ahmed.

The Süleymaniye is in the left foreground (1). To the right is the Ministry of War, where Mehmed the Conqueror's Old Palace (Eski Saray) once stood, and where Istanbul University stands today (2). Flanking it on the right is Beyazıt Square, overshadowed by the mosque of Sultan Bayezid II (3). The six minarets of the mosque of Sultan Ahmed clearly distinguish this edifice (4), located to the south, next to At Meydanı, site of the old hippodrome (5). To the left are Hagia Sophia (6) and Topkapı Palace (7), with the Sea of Marmara in the background (8).

Sultanahmet

The Mosque and Complex of
Sultan Ahmed I

Ahmet Vefa Çobanoğlu

The mosque of Sultan Ahmed I (*r.* 1603–17) is situated in the oldest part of Istanbul, in the neighbourhood of Sultanahmet, on the site of the hippodrome, a chariot racecourse and a hub of social and political life in ancient times. It is close to the Hagia Sophia, near the spot where the Great Palace of the Byzantine emperors once stood, and a short distance from Topkapı Sarayı, the abode of the Ottoman sultans.

The hippodrome was the heart of Byzantium. Inspired by Rome's Circus Maximus, it was first built after 196 CE, during the reign of Emperor Septimius Severius (*r.* 193–211), and reconstructed and enlarged under Constantine I (*r.* 323–37, as sole emperor). Replete with magnificent monuments, the hippodrome was the largest open area inside the city walls (about 45,000m^2), a place where important ceremonies were held. Besides chariot races, wild animal fights and other spectacles were staged here. The emperor's loge, reached from the (then) nearby Great Palace, occupied the southeast perimeter, most likely where the outer courtyard of Sultan Ahmed's mosque now stands.

The hippodrome was heavily damaged by earthquakes and riots over the centuries. Of the monuments that were located along its central axis, the *spina*, or 'spine', only three have survived: the Egyptian Obelisk, the Serpentine Column and a roughly built stone pillar, often referred to as the Column of Emperor Constantine VII Porphyrogenitus, although it predates his reign. During the Ottoman period, the hippodrome was cut in half and reorganised. In Turkish, it became known as At Meydanı, 'Square of Horses', because of its historical use for horse races, a name which still endures today.

Towering above this ancient locale, the mosque of Sultan Ahmed (Sultanahmet Camii) dominates the skyline. Popularly known as the 'Blue Mosque' (for a particular feature of its interior decoration), it is immediately recognisable by its distinctive six minarets. Designed by the architect Sedefkâr Mehmed Agha (*d.* post 1617), it was built between 1609 and 1617. Like Istanbul's other imperial mosques, it is surrounded by a

OPPOSITE
Panorama of the Sultanahmet neighbourhood, showing the mosque of Sultan Ahmed in the middle ground and Hagia Sophia and Topkapi Palace in the background. Almost the entire length of the hippodrome is visible on the left; the domes in the foreground mark the southern end of the ancient racecourse.

külliye, or complex of educational and charitable institutions, which was completed in 1620.

Soon after opening, the mosque of Sultan Ahmed replaced Hagia Sophia (which had been converted into a mosque following the conquest of Constantinople in 1453) as the primary location for official ceremonies, the sultan's Friday prayers and important celebrations, including the Mevlid Kandili, the annual commemoration of the Prophet Muhammad's birthday. It was also the scene of momentous events throughout Ottoman history.

In 1622, leaders of the religious hierarchy and the Janissaries (a corps of professional infantrymen in the Ottoman army) gathered here to launch an uprising against Sultan Osman II (*r*. 1618–22), Ahmed I's son, which led to his dethronement and assassination. Two centuries later, when Mahmud II (*r*. 1808–39) acted decisively to eliminate the Janissaries, who had become corrupt and ineffective militarily, the sacred standard of the Prophet Muhammad (Sancak-ı Şerif) was unfurled in the mosque, to unite the sultan's loyal subjects in a holy struggle against the corps. Weary of Janissary excesses, the populace of Istanbul heeded this call and played a crucial role in the destruction of the unruly soldiery, an episode known to history as the Auspicious Incident (1826).

Today, the mosque of Sultan Ahmed is not only one of Istanbul's most important places of worship, but a world-renowned architectural monument. The surrounding area, Sultanahmet, which takes its name from the mosque, is both a vibrant tourist centre and the site of religious celebrations, cultural festivals and many other events in the daily life of the city – much as it has been over the course of two millennia.

Economics and Location

The Ottoman Empire reached the peak of its power and territorial extent during the 1500s, under Süleyman I (*r*. 1520–

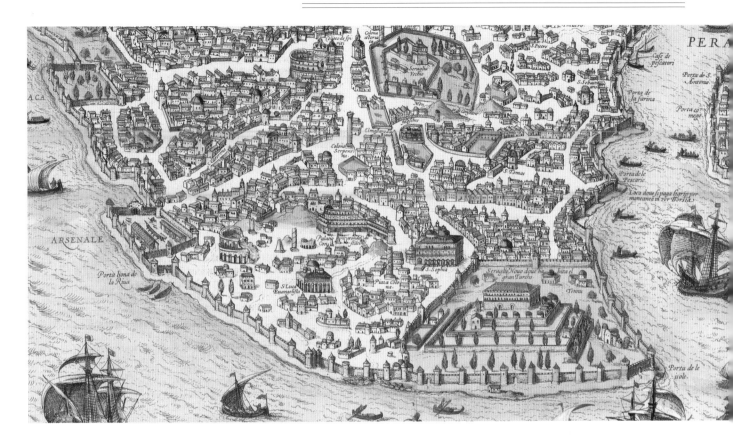

66), but it began to wane in the following century. When Ahmed I ascended the throne, the Ottomans were at war on two fronts, with the Safavids of Persia in the east and the Habsburgs in the west. Safavid armies seized Revan, Kars and other major cities, while the Habsburgs made inroads in Hungary. Simultaneously, rebellions erupted in Anatolia and elsewhere, creating internal upheaval. Beginning in 1607, Grand Vizier Kuyucu ('the well-sinker') Murad Pasha (*d.* 1611) systematically crushed these revolts with military force.

Despite this turmoil, the Ottoman Empire remained a crucial market for Europeans, and commerce with Europe flourished. During Ahmed I's reign, the Ottomans renewed bilateral agreements, or capitulations, with Britain, France and Venice,

BELOW
Historic nineteenth-century photograph of At Meydanı and the mosque of Sultan Ahmed.

which granted their subjects trading privileges in the imperial realm. Merchants of Spain, Portugal, Catalonia and various Italian states also engaged in commerce in the empire, but under the French flag. In 1612, a pact was made with Holland, then the rising star of Europe's maritime trade. The capitulations became a burden on the empire in later centuries, but in the 1600s they served Ottoman political interests and provided essential income for the central treasury, especially customs revenues.

In times past, construction of Istanbul's imperial mosques and complexes had been financed mainly by wealth won from conquests in foreign lands. Sultan Ahmed lacked this source of capital, and his mosque and *külliye* were the first that were erected entirely with resources from the treasury. Significant funds from the state's coffers were also spent to acquire the land on which they were built.

During the fifteenth and sixteenth centuries, when the spoils of victory paid for construction, a number of large-scale mosques and complexes were constructed in Istanbul. In the 1600s, except for the mosque of Sultan Ahmed and the Yeni Valide Camii (Yenicami, or New Mosque), in Eminönü, the Ottomans did not build grand edifices in the capital. (Sultan Ahmed's grandmother, Safiye Sultan (*d.* 1605) began erecting the latter mosque in 1597, but the project was halted in 1603 and only completed in 1663.)

Istanbul's population had grown considerably by the seventeenth century. Little land was left for monumental structures, and confiscating it was expensive. Rather than undertaking large, costly projects on the city's densely inhabited peninsula, the Ottomans built major buildings in the empire's provinces, particularly along the route from the capital to the Hijaz and Mecca. (Two important examples from the 1600s are the *külliyes* of Okuz Mehmed Pasha at Ulukışla, Niğde and Kara Mustafa Pasha at İncesu, Kayseri.)

In Istanbul, viziers, pashas, and other high-ranking officials erected a number of smaller buildings during the 1600s, which were essentially *külliyes* centred around *medreses* (schools). Previously, mosques had been at the core of such complexes, but the more modest *külliyes* of this era were often built around schools.

The site of the ancient hippodrome, At Meydanı, had also become highly desirable property by the seventeenth century. Within a decade of the Ottoman Conquest, Sultan Mehmed II (*r.* 1444–6 and 1451–81) had begun building a palace near here – Saray-ı Cedid-i Amire, 'the Imperial New Palace', later known

as Topkapı Sarayı. At the end of the fifteenth century, the Firuz Ağa Mosque, mausoleum and school were erected in the same vicinity, followed by the palace of Ibrahim Pasha, Süleyman I's famous grand vizier. Moreover, At Meydanı was the setting for major celebrations and events, many of which are illustrated in Turkish miniature paintings. Sultan Murad III's (r. 1574–95) lavish 53-day circumcision ceremony for Şehzade (Prince) Mehmed, between 7 June and 30 July 1582, is one of the most famous.

Roughly three decades later, Sultan Ahmed I chose this key location – prominent both in past and present – as the site for the mosque and *külliye* that would be his legacy. The complex he erected would redefine the area and distinguish it for centuries to come.

Layout of the Mosque and Complex
See the plan on the inside back cover

The mosque and *külliye* of Sultan Ahmed lack symmetrical relationship. Topography, plots of obtainable land and existing monuments in the hippodrome dictated the design of the complex. The *külliye* comprised diverse educational, charitable, commercial and other buildings: an imperial kiosk (*hünkâr kasrı*), a market (*arasta*), bath (*hamam*), primary scool for boys (*sıbyan mektebi*), theological school (*medrese*), the mausoleum (*türbe*) of Ahmed I, a Qur'an readers' room (*darülkurra*), hospital (*darüşşifa*, with its own bath and small mosque), soup kitchen (*imaret*), hospices (*tabhaneler*), kiosks from which water was distributed to the public (*sebiller*), fountains (*çeşmeler*), shops and houses. Many of these structures are no longer extant.

Although the buildings appear scattered, they create a functional whole. The mosque and the *hünkâr kasrı* attached to it on the southeast corner are located in a broad external courtyard. South of this court is the *arasta*, a row of shops which stretches along the entire length of the complex. A *hamam*,

OPPOSITE
A European artist's depiction of At Meydanı and Sultan Ahmed's mosque, which takes some creative license with perspective.

OVERLEAF
View of the mosque of Sultan Ahmed, looking towards Istanbul's Asian shore across the Bosphorus. The small square domed building on the left edge of the image, in the middle ground, is the sultan's mausoleum.

as well as a *sebil*, lay at the southwest end of the market. The *sıbyan mektebi* is situated on the east side of the courtyard, and the *medrese* is located to the north, abutting the east wall of the outer court. Beside it, flanking At Meydanı, are the türbe of Ahmed I and the *darülkurra*, surrounded by a separate wall.

Previously, a *sebil* stood adjacent to the tomb, in the corner that overlooks the square. Today, this space is occupied by a building that was erected to serve as a *muvakkithane*, or 'place for the prayer service timekeeper'. Several shops, the entrance gates to the outer court and *sebils* are situated on the north side of the complex. To the southwest, in the direction of the Sea of Marmara, at the rounded southern end (sphendone) of the hippodrome was the *darüşşifa*. The buildings of the *imaret*, including the *tabhaneler*, were also situated here. Only the structures that housed the *imaret*'s kitchen, oven, pantry and dining hall have survived to the present.

RIGHT
Sultan Ahmed's mosque from the southeast. The structure over the vaulted passage (foreground) is the imperial kiosk, and the steps below lead to the *arasta*.

The Mosque

THE OUTER COURTYARD

A number of entrances lead into the outer court (*dış avlu*) that encloses the mosque's forecourt and prayer hall. The north and east sides of this expansive precinct have three gates each, and the west and south have two apiece. The east entrances also provide access to the *darülkurra*, *medrese* and *sıbyan mektebi* situated on this side of the court. The paths through the south gates, on either side of the prayer hall, climb up the slope from the *arasta* and neighbourhood below. The entryways on the west side of the court have been sealed up.

The gates on the north wall, which open to the mosque's grounds from At Meydanı, are grander than those on the other sides of the outer courtyard. The central entrance has survived intact since the seventeenth century. Those to the right and left, on the same wall, are flanked by *sebils* and have upper floors constructed of stone and brick, which formerly served as quarters for the mosque's personnel.

All of the outer courtyard's walls, except for the north, are composed of dressed coarse sandstone. The north wall is made of marble, which accentuates its primacy as the main periphery, bordering At Meydanı.

THE MINARETS

Sultanahmet Camii is the first and only Ottoman mosque with six minarets. Those located at the four corners of the building have three balconies (*şerefes*) each, while the smaller pair at the north end of the inner court have two apiece. Like most of the mosque's other structures, they are made of *küfeki*, a durable type of sandstone, which was frequently used from ancient times through the Ottoman period for monumental buildings in Istanbul.

The minarets' fluted shafts are richly adorned with *mukarnas* corbels, which hang honeycomb-like below the delicately carved

geometric openwork railings of the *şerefes*. (Often defined as 'stalactites', *mukarnas* is a common type of architectural decoration found throughout the central and eastern parts of the Muslim world.) Stylised cypress motifs embellish the smaller minarets, while a band of turquoise tiles encircles the bodies of those at the corners of the prayer hall, directly below their caps. The garlands in relief around the upper parts of the north minarets were added during renovations, following damage by an earthquake in 1894.

During Ramadan (the ninth month of the Islamic calendar, when Muslims fast) and other special occasions, strings of lights spelling out pious epigrams are suspended between the two minarets on the east side of the mosque. This tradition, known as *mahya*, dates back to Ottoman times, when oil lamps were used for illumination. Today, the lights are powered by electricity.

The mosque's atypical number of minarets has given rise to many legends. One claims that Sultan Ahmed ordered Sedefkâr Mehmed Agha to build minarets of gold. The architect knew that this was impossible, but to avoid challenging the ruler directly, he erected six minarets. Later, when the sultan asked why his order had not been implemented, Mehmed Agha replied that he had misunderstood and constructed six (*altı*) minarets instead of making them out of gold (*altın*).

THE INNER COURTYARD

The porticoed forecourt (*iç avlu*, or *harem*, in the sense of inviolable space) is slightly larger than the mosque's prayer hall. Its outer east and west façades consist of two-storey galleries, which is unique in Ottoman architecture and resembles the pattern on the adjacent sides of the prayer hall. Water taps for ablutions are arranged in a row in the lower gallery, while the upper section opens to the outside through a line of pointed arches between smaller round ones. Huge gates provide access to the courtyard on three sides.

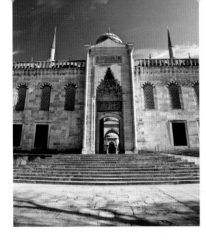

Recessed arches embellished with alternating red and white voussoirs and flanking marble niches encrusted with *mukarnas* animate the inner faces of these entrances. The external façade of the east gate is crowned with an eight-line inscription, while its counterpart on the opposite side of the court lacks calligraphy.

A lofty, domed portal with a stalactite semi-dome (on the exterior side) distinguishes the north entryway from those on the east and west façades. The top, outer face of this main gate (*taç kapı*) is inscribed with the Islamic profession of faith: 'There is no god but God, and Muhammad is the Messenger of God'. A second inscription appears below the vault of the semi-dome, displaying a portion of verse 103 of the Qur'an's Surat al-Nisaa (Chapter of the Women): '... Worship at fixed times hath been enjoined on the believers'. Inside, on the courtyard face, a plaque over the entrance is emblazoned with a compatible passage, verses 34–35 of Surat al-Ma'arij (Chapter of the Ascending Stairways): 'And those that are attentive at their worship/ These will dwell in Gardens, honoured'. A sundial, to indicate prayer times, is carved in the stone below and to the right of this inscription.

The leaves of the huge bronze doors in all three of the forecourt's entrances exhibit superb workmanship. Those in the *taç kapı* are particularly attractive. Part of the thirteenth verse of the Qur'an's Surat al-Saff (Chapter of the Ranks) is inscribed above the exquisite geometric designs engraved on the leaves: '... help from Allah and present victory. Give good tidings (O Muhammad) to believers'. The well-known Turkish chronicler Evliya Çelebi (1611–82) recounts in his *Seyahatname*, 'Narrative of Travels', that his father, Derviş Mehmed Zilli, a master jeweller at the Ottoman court, made the leaves for the courtyard's main door.

Geometric patterns in coloured stone break the monotony of the forecourt's white marble pavement tiles, both next to the north gate and in front of the prayer hall's main door (*cümle kapısı*) directly opposite. The varying red and white voussoirs of the arches in the portico on the building's north façade, the

OPPOSITE
The forecourt, overshadowed by a minaret with three balconies.

TOP
The *taç kapı*, the main, north entrance to the mosque's inner courtyard.

ABOVE
A stalactite semi-dome and calligraphy embellish the north gate.

BELOW
The inner court in Ottoman times
(W. H. Bartlett, 1838).

so-called 'latecomers' gallery', or *son cemaat yeri* (capped by nine domes), and the domed colonnade (*revak*) that surrounds the rest of the court, add further vitality to the space.

A cistern lies beneath the courtyard, and a hexagonal marble pool occupies its centre. Although it resembles an ablution fountain (*şadırvan*), this pool is purely decorative. The arches that carry its dome are embellished with a variety of patterns in relief – floral designs and, on the voussoirs, *rumis* (abstract ornaments resembling leaves, frequently found in Turkish decorative arts, which developed from zoomorphic motifs).

The 238th verse of Surat al-Baqarah (Chapter of the Cow) appears above the central arch of the latecomers' gallery, on the mosque's north façade: 'Be guardians of your prayers, and of the midmost prayer, and stand up with devotion to Allah'. Inscriptions of seven lines each also crown the stalactite niches on either side of the prayer hall's main door, which is topped by a calligraphic plaque containing the names of Sultan Ahmed I and all his predecessors, extending back to the founder of the Ottoman dynasty, Osman I (*d.* 1324).

ABOVE
Even in the past, the pool in the forecourt was simply a decorative element rather than a place for performing ablutions, as evidenced by this nineteenth-century photograph.

RIGHT
The prayer hall of the mosque of Sultan Ahmed, looking towards the *mihrap*.

RIGHT
The prayer hall, view to the
southwest, showing one of the
massive pillars ('elephant's feet')
that supports the central dome.

OPPOSITE
Galleries on the east side of the
prayer hall.

OVERLEAF
The central dome rises 43 metres
above the ground.

THE PRAYER HALL

The fundamental layout of the mosque of Sultan Ahmed, a prayer hall fronted by a porticoed forecourt, is typical of classical Ottoman architecture. The *cümle kapısı* serves as the primary entrance to the prayer hall, and four more doorways (two on each side of the building) provide access from the outer courtyard. Silver, ivory, mother-of-pearl and tortoiseshell inlay work in geometric shapes embellishes the wooden leaves of the doors.

The prayer hall is nearly square (64 x 72 metres), and its central dome, which measures 22.4 metres in diameter (inside), rests on four pointed arches and pendentives. The four massive pillars (*fil ayak*, or 'elephant feet') that support the arches dominate the interior space. Convex flutes in the marble bases of the pillars that carry the dome soften their bulk (5 metres in diameter), and those on the north are adorned with elegant marble fountains (*çeşmes*). Buttressing arches that connect the pillars to piers in the walls serve to distribute the tremendous load of the dome outward, equally on all sides. The pillars are reflected on the building's exterior by octagonal domed weight towers that extend from the huge supports onto the roof above. Small buttresses on these towers also help reinforce the dome.

The central dome (43 metres high) is surrounded by four half-domes, which are ringed by exedrae – three on each side, except the south, which has two. Resembling a quatrefoil, this centralised plan provides a spacious, open interior. Mimar Sinan (*c.* 1490–1588) created the prototype, which is evident in his first large-scale work, the Şehzade Mosque, in Istanbul's Fatih district. In 1597, Chief Architect Davud Agha (*d.* 1599), one of Sinan's pupils, applied the same design for the Yeni Valide Mosque in Eminönü, and another of Sinan's students, Dalgıç Ahmed Agha (*d.* 1607), preserved the pattern, until work on this building was suspended in 1603. In turn, Sedefkâr Mehmed Agha employed the plan for Sultan Ahmed's mosque, but with some elaborations, such as the exedrae, which extend the

quatrefoil's dimensions and produce an even more expansive interior.

The middle of the central dome is splendidly adorned with the forty-first verse of Qur'an's Surat al-Fatir (Chapter of the Creator): 'Lo! Allah graspeth the heavens and the earth that they deviate not, and if they were to deviate there is not one that could grasp them after Him. Lo! He is ever Clement, Forgiving'. Below, towards the base of the drum, the thirty-fifth verse of Surat al-Nur (Chapter of the Light), which begins 'Allah is the Light of the heavens and the earth...', wraps around the space above the row of windows.

Qur'anic verses are also inscribed in the half-domes and on the exedrae beside them, as well as on the four great pillars that carry the main dome. The pendentives display calligraphic medallions composed of the ninety-nine most beautiful names of God (*al-asma' al-husna*). Ottoman sources record that the renowned calligrapher Seyyid Kasim Gubari (*d.* 1624) was responsible for many of the mosque's magnificent inscriptions, which also include a number of plaques hanging on the walls.

Galleries bordered by marble railings laced with openwork foliate designs frame all sides of the prayer hall's interior, except for the south, where the *mihrap* is located – the niche in the wall that indicates the *kıble*, or the direction of Mecca, towards which Muslims pray. The alternating red and white voussoirs that fill the arches of the galleries replicate the pattern of the *revak* in the forecourt. An abundance of windows, many of which are brilliantly tinted with stained glass, floods the mosque with light; those on the *mihrap* wall are especially striking.

Outside the prayer hall, two large buttresses divide the arched galleries that stretch along the building's exterior east and west façades into three sections. (This arrangement is mirrored by the galleries inside, which are partitioned by the piers that protrude from the walls into the interior space.) The north sections of the outer galleries consist of a single level, while those in the middle and on the south (capped by three domes) have two floors. The façades display architectural vigour that is conspicuously missing in the static, bulky exterior of the nearby Hagia Sophia.

Compared to the east and west sides of the mosque, the outer face of the (south) *kıble* wall is plain. A vaulted lower-level area at this end of the building was probably used to stable the mounts of the sultan and his entourage when they came to attend prayers. It is now part of a carpet and *kilim* museum operated by the General Directorate of Pious Foundations.

FURNISHINGS AND DECORATION

The carved floral motifs and coloured stone inlay on the mosque's marble *mihrap* make it one of the finest examples of a prayer niche from the early seventeenth century. It is flanked by two pairs of silver candlesticks, one large, one small, holding beeswax candles. The inscriptions above the niche are Qur'anic passages that are traditionally used at this location in mosques, from the thirty-seventh and thirty-ninth verses of Surat Al-i-'Imran (Chapter of the Family of 'Imran). The gilded marble *minber* (the high dais to the right of the *mihrap*, for the imam to deliver an address during the Friday prayer) is also ornamented with exquisite carving, in foliate and geometric patterns.

Verse 277 of the Qur'an's Surat al-Baqarah (Chapter of the Cow) appears on the wall over the *mihrap*, in a band above the three windows: 'Lo! those who believe and do good works and establish worship and pay the poor-due, their reward is with

their Lord and there shall no fear come upon them, neither shall they grieve'. An octagonal medallion in angular Kufic script, the oldest type of Arabic calligraphy, is set into the masonry to the left of the prayer niche. Beneath it, there is a tablet of coloured stone.

Legend recounts that this panel was the dining table of Veysel Karani (Uways al-Qarani in Arabic, *d.* 657), a venerated figure in Sufism, Islam's mystical dimension, whose reported communication with the Prophet Muhammad through dreams and visions forms the basis of the tradition of the Uwaysiyya, a group of mystics who look for guidance from the spirits of departed or physically absent individuals. Supposedly, the

**ABOVE
LEFT**
The *mihrap* and *minber*.

RIGHT
Detail of the foliate motifs that
decorate the *minber*.

table has curative powers, and people seeking relief from their infirmities sometimes touch the stone or pray in front of it.

Next to the southeast pillar, to the left of the *mihrap*, a recently restored wooden *kürsü* (raised seat for an imam), exquisitely inlaid with mother-of-pearl, presents a splendid example of the craft of *kündekari* ('tongue-and-groove joining'), in which small pieces of wood are fitted together in geometric shapes without glue or nails. (Many of the mosque's doors and windows were fashioned with the same technique.) By comparison, the prayer hall's two other *kürsüs* are austere. One, near the east gallery, is quite plain, while the other, beside the southwest pillar, is simply engraved with baroque motifs.

BELOW
The *kürsü* by the southeast pillar is richly inlaid with mother-of-pearl.

A tribune for muezzins (givers of the call to prayer) on ten octagonal marble columns adjoins the pillar to the right of the *mihrap*. Access to the platform is through a door next to the pillar. The black banner hanging from a staff above the left railing was presented to the mosque by the late Egyptian president Anwar Sadat. It is a replica of the standard used by Muslim forces at the Battle of Badr (624 CE), a key engagement

in the early days of Islam, when the followers of the new faith won a decisive victory over their pagan foes. The wooden cupboards below the muezzins' platform are painted in a customary style of the seventeenth century.

The *hünkâr mahfili*, or sultan's loge, where the ruler and his entourage prayed separately, is on the south wall, to the left of the *mihrap*. It is reached from outside the prayer hall, through the imperial kiosk (*hünkâr kasrı*), at the southeast corner of the building. Pointed arches on ten columns support the L-shaped platform, which is enclosed by a railing.

The loge has its own *mihrap*, as well as abundant ornamentation: Iznik tiles, variegated stonework, inlaid woodwork and calligraphy, including a rare example of a tiled inscription in a monumental form of Arabic script known as *celi sülüs*. The inscription's glistening panels embossed with gilt lettering on a turquoise field wind around the space like a sash. Besides Qur'anic verses, the inscriptions in the loge contain tributes to Ahmed I. One, engraved with the year 1616, indicates the structure's completion date.

To the left of the loge's *mihrap*, behind a window, is a small unadorned cell for fasting and seclusion (*çilehane*). Such rooms were generally used by dervishes of Islamic mystic sects for religious retirement and fasts, and they are rare in large, traditional Ottoman mosques. Reportedly, another place for spiritual isolation exists under the building, which is reached from imperial loge by a secret passageway. During the fasting month of Ramadan, the sultan apparently retreated to this room for ten days, where he would break his daily fasts with only a glass of water and a piece of bread.

In the main area of the prayer hall, the walls between the first and third row of windows are adorned with a luminous array of tiles. Over 21,000 embellish this space. Outside of Topkapı Palace, the mosque of Sultan Ahmed has the greatest number of tiles in any comparable Ottoman building. They are of a type manufactured using the 'underglaze' technique (where painted decoration is applied to the surface, glazed, and then fired to fix

the design) in the Anatolian cities of Iznik and Kütahya during the second half of the sixteenth century and first quarter of the seventeenth. Indeed, the historical development of tiles from these major contemporary production centres can be traced on the walls of the mosque.

More than 50 different compositions are evident in the prayer hall's tiles. Those with representations of cypresses or arrangements of medallions or sunbursts offer superb examples of coral red tiles characteristic of the sixteenth century. Most of the designs take motifs from the natural world, but some are purely abstract, such as those displaying *çintemani*, a popular pattern of three pearls with pairs of rippling stripes. Gardens are a foremost Islamic symbol of Paradise, and the numerous tiles with floral and vegetal designs evoke the notion of Eternity.

Tiles displaying similar compositions are often framed together, but their designs do not correlate to the panels bordering them, creating asymmetrical patterns on the walls. Besides coral red, the most frequently used colours are blue, green and turquoise, primarily on a white background. The various motifs on the tiles – hyacinths, carnations, tulips, chrysanthemums, flowering spring branches, *hatayi* (an intricate combination of flowers and leaves) and many more – appear commonly in other Turkish arts of the period.

Above the mosque's third row of windows, the space is embellished with *kalem işi* (polychrome wall painting made with a brush, or *kalem*, on various surfaces, including plaster, wood and stone). During renovations in 1883, the existing decoration was covered in whitewash, and though fresh painting was done, the dimensions and details of the original patterns were lost. Moreover, the new colour scheme was unbecoming – various tones of blue on a light blue background. The resulting predominant hue also earned the building a new name. This, not the colour of its tiles, is the reason why the mosque of Sultan Ahmed became known as the Blue Mosque.

During restorations that began in 1976, original designs in the building's upper space were uncovered and preserved or restored. Despite the renovators' best efforts, variations in colour and motif occurred. Red and light blue prevail in the renewed decoration. Examples of original *kalem işi* can be observed on the wooden ceiling under the imperial loge and on the leaves of the wooden cupboards beneath the müezzins' tribune.

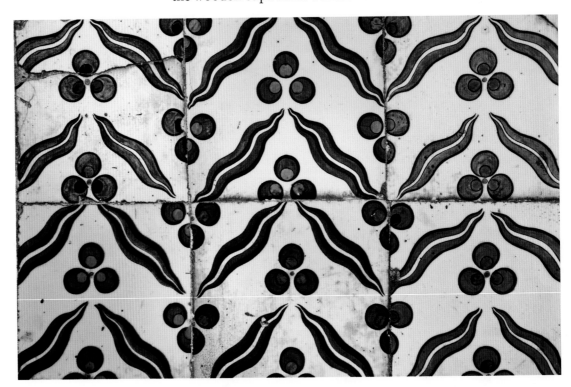

ABOVE
The *çintemani* pattern on a section of Iznik tiles.

THE IMPERIAL KIOSK

The imperial kiosk, or *hünkâr kasrı*, an L-shaped, two-storey structure, is located at the southeast corner of the mosque. The walls of the lower floor are made of dressed coarse sandstone (*küfeki*), while those on the upper floor display alternating rows of stone and brick; the baroque marble fountain on the north wall is a later addition. The building is entered by a ramp from the outer courtyard, and it is connected to the mosque and to the imperial loge inside. The kiosk offered a place for the sultan to rest before and after prayer services, as well as to attend to matters of business.

This *hünkâr kasrı* is the first example in Ottoman architecture. Subsequently, such kiosks became a standard component of imperial mosques, and they were even added to existing edifices.

One of the most striking examples is at Eminönü's Yeni Valide Camii. It was severely damaged by fire in 1912, but later restored to its original state. Currently, the *hünkâr kasrı* at the mosque of Sultan Ahmed is part of the carpet and *kilim* museum run by the General Directorate of Pious Foundations.

Construction of the Mosque

When Sultan Ahmed I ascended the throne in 1603, he planned to finish building the Yeni Valide Camii in Eminönü, which had been started by his grandmother, Safiye Sultan, six years earlier and remained half-finished. Later, he decided to erect a mosque in his own name and selected the south side of At Meydanı as the location. This area was not only a centre of public life, with many important buildings, but commanded a prominent position on the city's skyline, especially when viewed from the Sea of Marmara. The silhouette of Hagia Sophia stood out on this vista, and a majestic new mosque nearby would enhance the panorama.

Situated next to At Meydanı, the mosque would also integrate with the large open area of the old hippodrome, and the buildings of the *külliye* would create a new order around this space, complementing and completing the whole. Five Ottoman palaces already occupied the site and had to be acquired from their owners, who were paid compensation. The sum of 30,000 gold pieces spent for one, the palace of Ayşe Sultan, hints at the tremendous cost of confiscating property in this vicinity. After expropriation, the palaces were razed.

Sedefkâr Mehmed Agha then outlined a plan that delineated the position of the mosque's walls, its minarets and the piers to carry its dome, as well as the location of the imperial loge and the *mihrap* (a niche inside mosques that designates the direction of Mecca). On 8 October 1609, labourers broke ground for the trenches to hold the foundations.

From the outset of construction, the sultan, various government officials and other notables including the *şeyhülislam* (chief religious authority in the Ottoman state) and the leaders of the foremost dervish lodges, observed the work from a special pavilion. On occasion, some would pick up tools and, reciting prayers, join the labourers. At times, even the sultan took part in the backbreaking effort, toiling until he perspired and became weary. (His pickaxe is inventoried in the Topkapı Palace

Museum collection. Roughly a century later, Sultan Ahmed III (*r.* 1704–39) used the same tool to help excavate the ground for the foundations of his library in Topkapı Palace's third court.)

Legend records that the blessed Hızır, revered in Islam as a messenger of God, appeared to Ahmed I one day during construction and asked, 'O sultan, who will pray in this mosque, so close to Hagia Sophia?'

Somewhat perplexed, the ruler replied that children would come, if no one else.

OPPOSITE
European engraving of the mosque of Sultan Ahmed, with all the architectural elements labelled. The quatrefoil design of the domical structure is depicted clearly.

'Yes', answered Hızır, 'children will come and play here'.

When the sultan realised that he was speaking to the blessed Hızır, he immediately took him by the arm. 'Promise that you will come here to pray at least once a day', he said, 'or I will not let you go'.

Hızır agreed, and over the following centuries, many who believed this account supposedly came to Sultan Ahmed's mosque every day in the hope of seeing this servant of God during one of the five daily prayers.

The trenches for the mosque's foundations had been dug by the end of December 1609, and, with accompanying ceremony and prayer, the first stones were laid in January 1610. After the crowds dispersed, the sultan climbed down to the level of the foundations and placed several stones on the spot where the *mihrap* would stand, for the sake of providence.

Seven years later, on Friday 9 June 1617, the mosque opened for worship and a celebratory feast was held. Evliya Çelebi reported that a number of rulers and other important persons presented gifts for the occasion, most notably the Ottoman governor of Abyssinia, Cafer Pasha, who sent six emerald lamps with gold chains.

Since the mosque's construction register was signed by Sultan Mustafa I, after Ahmed I had passed away on 22 November 1617, the final fixtures were presumably put in place after the latter's death. The rest of the buildings in the *külliye* were completed one after the other, by 1620.

The Other Structures of the Complex

East of the mosque, and flanking the wall of the outer court, is a *sıbyan mektebi*, or primary school for boys, which was probably completed in 1617. Square in plan and composed of dressed coarse sandstone, it stands above ground on a double-vaulted under-structure. The school was heavily damaged by fire in 1912 and refurbished in 1965. Shops once occupied the space near the

LELEVATION ET LE PLAN DE LA MOSQVÉE DE SVLTAN ACHMED ·

(now restored) marble fountain beside the entrance.

A *medrese* (theological school), most likely erected in 1620, is located to the northeast of the mosque. The building consists of 24 domed rooms fronted by a domed colonnade around a rectangular court, which was originally open but later roofed over. Students were educated here in *hadis* (Ar. *hadith*), sayings and actions attributed to the Prophet Muhammad, which, along with the Qur'an, form the basis of Islamic jurisprudence. The *medrese* has been repaired at various times, most recently in 1935; it is used today by the Turkish Republic Prime Ministry's Directorate of Ottoman Archives.

Sultan Ahmed I's mausoleum (*türbe*) and a *darülkurra*, or Qur'an reading room (probably completed in 1620), occupy a separate courtyard to the north of the *medrese*. An arched opening in the *darülkurra* allowed one to gaze into the mausoleum, especially on the sultan's coffin, in the middle of the back row. The Qur'an was recited continuously in this room, to gladden the souls of the ruler and others who lay beside him. The *darülkurra*'s dome is decorated with floral motifs and inscribed

BELOW
Sultan Ahmed's mausoleum,
where 35 other members of the
Ottoman house also rest.

with chapter 112 of the Qur'an, the Unity Chapter (Surat al-Ikhlas).

Sultan Ahmed I's *türbe* is one of the most beautiful buildings in the complex. Construction of this domed mausoleum commenced after the ruler's death and concluded in 1619, during the reign of Osman II. The exterior façade is covered in marble, and the interior is richly embellished. An oyster-shell pediment crowns the construction epigraph over the entryway. Inlaid with ivory, mother-of-pearl and silver, the ebony-encased leaves of the door are engraved with the supplication, 'O Opener of the gates (God)/ Open for us the gates of auspiciousness'.

Floral designs on shimmering Iznik tiles adorn the inner chamber from the floor to the top of the lower row of windows. The medallion in the centre of the dome displays the forty-first

verse of the Qur'an's Surat al-Fatir (Chapter of the Creator), and the pendentives are ornamented with the ninety-nine most beautiful names of God (*al-asma' al-husna*). The zigzag painted decoration (*kalem işi*) inside the dome and on the walls next to the second tier of windows mirrors the patterns of calligraphy on the coverings that drape the coffins below. A band of blue tiles inscribed with white *sülüs* calligraphy, which encircles the chamber between the first and second rows of windows, displays the verses of Surat al-Mulk (The Sovereignty Chapter) of the Qur'an. Lines of poetry eulogizing Sultan Osman II are inscribed in the niches in the walls on the far side of the chamber.

The *türbe* contains 36 coffins, including those of Ahmed I's wife, Mahpeyker Kösem Sultan, and the sultans Osman II and Murad IV. The marble inscription shaped like an arch on the wall above Murad IV's coffin comprises seven lines of poetry composed by the ruler himself. Three graves are also located outside the mausoleum, near the courtyard wall.

The *arasta*, to the south of the mosque, consists of a long row of facing shops, completed in 1617. In the past, as many as 200 shops were located in the market, but today there are only about 80. The great fire of 1912 destroyed much of the *arasta*. It was restored between 1982 and 1985 and opened as a tourist bazaar.

Excavations carried out in the market, in 1935–38 and 1951–54, uncovered floor mosaics from the Great Palace of the Byzantine emperors, which occupied this area in ancient times. They can be viewed in the Mosaic Museum, which was built around the remains and replaced some of the *arasta*'s shops. Besides this market, commercial spaces existed in other parts of the *külliye*. Those along the wall of the outer court, facing At Meydanı, still function as shops today.

The *hamam* at the southwest edge of the *arasta* was probably also completed in 1617, when the market was built. It has been in ruins since the fire of 1912. Filled with rubble, the bath's warm room (*ılıklık*) and hot room (*sıcaklık*) are evident, along with the boiler room and part of the reservoir. The cold room (*soğukluk*), which had a wooden façade, was completely destroyed by the

ABOVE
The *arasta*, a marketplace that served the local populace in Ottoman times, has become a busy tourist bazaar today.

OPPOSITE
At Meydanı in the Ottoman era (Thomas Allom, 1838).

fire. The hexagonal plan of the building's hot room resembles Mimar Sinan's design for the *hamam* at the Kılıç Ali Paşa Complex in Istanbul's Tophane area.

The *külliye*'s hospital, or *darüşşifa*, and most of the structures of the adjacent soup kitchen (*imaret*), which were located at the western end of At Meydanı and completed in 1620, no longer exist. The *darüşşifa*, which was arranged around a square court with a portico, had its own bath and small mosque. Only a

door on the east side of the *hamam* and the marble spout of a pool that was in the centre of the courtyard are still extant. The hospital continued to function until the middle of the nineteenth century, when it was replaced by a trade school, which opened in 1866. Today, part of the Sultanahmet Industrial Professions Lycée occupies the present building.

The *imaret*, which was begun in 1616 and probably finished in 1620, occupied the space in front of the hospital. The only remains of this large institution are structural traces of the kitchen, oven, pantry and dining hall. The hospices (*tabhaneler*) have not survived. In 1889, the Italian architect Raimondo D'Aranco, one the most important representatives in Istanbul of the Art Nouveau movement, erected a building for the Ministry of Agriculture (Ziraat Nezareti) on the site where the hospice once stood. Today, this imposing edifice serves as the rector's office of Marmara University.

The *külliye* of Sultan Ahmed originally had eight *sebils*, or kiosks for distributing water freely to the public. Today, only five

101. Mosquée Ahmed.

ABOVE
Late nineteenth-century
photograph of At Meydanı and
the mosque of Sultan Ahmed.
The *sebil* next to the east gate on
the north wall of the outer court
is visible behind the trees.

OPPOSITE
The *sebil* by the north wall's west
gate.

are evident, in various states of preservation. The root meaning
of the word *sebil* (*sabil* in Arabic) is 'way' or 'path'. From the
notion of performing charity 'in the path of God' (*fi sabil Allah*),
the term eventually acquired the further meaning of a place for
public water supply provided by someone's benevolence.

The best preserved *sebils* are connected to the east and west
gates on the north wall of the outer courtyard. In former times,
attendants would have distributed water (and even sherbet
and lemonade on special occasions) from the large iron-grilled
windows on both sides of these buildings. A four-line inscription
by the window of the *sebil* beside the east gate, on the façade

overlooking At Meydanı, mentions the architect Mehmed Agha and the date of construction, 1617. Presumably, the kiosk next to the west gate, which lacks a dedication, was built in the same year. A *sebil* at the east end of the *arasta* was also erected in 1617, and another, at the opposite end of the market, of which there are scant traces, was probably constructed two years earlier.

Sebils also existed at one time on the north and south walls of the court surrounding the mausoleum of Ahmed I, facing At Meydanı and the *medrese* respectively. The *türbe*'s interior was visible through the windows, allowing recipients of water to view the coffin of their benefactor, upon whose soul they undoubtedly asked God's blessing. Another *sebil* was located at the northeast side of the mausoleum, where the *muvakkithane* now stands. Evliya Çelebi also recounts that a water kiosk was situated near the hospital and soup kitchen, but its exact location is unknown.

Besides *sebils*, the complex of Sultan Ahmed had nine *çeşmes*, or mural fountains (a kind of 'self-service' water source usually composed of a rectangular vertical panel with a recessed niche fit with a tap over a protruding basin, carved from marble). Six of these exist in places that were part of the *külliye*'s original plan, including the outer court, near the *arasta* and inside the mosque – on the north pillars that support the dome. During the nineteenth century, one of the *arasta*'s shops was converted into a fountain. The *çeşme* by the *sıbyan mektebi* was renovated completely in 1965, and the fountain on the façade of the imperial kiosk was placed there in 1979.

Several large spaces linked in a row under the south wall of the outer court were probably constructed as water depots. A nearby Byzantine ruin that was connected to these spaces might have served as a *gasilhane*, or a place for ritually washing the dead. There is also a square pool on the south side of the mosque, presumably added in the early nineteenth century to provide water in the event of fire.

Sultan Ahmed I

Ahmed I, the son of Sultan Mehmed III (*r.* 1595–1603) and
Handan Sultan (*d.* 1605), was born in Manisa in 1590 and
ascended the throne on 22 December 1603, at the age of 14.
He was the fourteenth ruler of the Ottoman dynasty. Devoutly

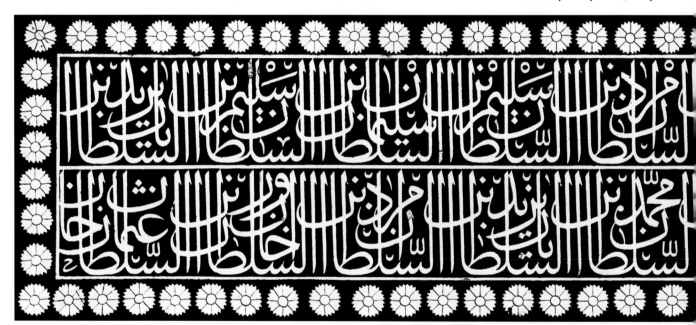

ABOVE
Calligraphic plaque above the
main entrance to the prayer hall,
which is engraved with the names
of Sultan Ahmed and all the
rulers of the Ottoman dynasty
back to its founder, Osman I.

religious, he soon won the trust of his subjects by dedicating
himself to scholarship and piety rather than to pleasure-seeking.
Unlike his predecessors, he did not participate personally in
military campaigns. He was fond of hunting, as well as *cirit*, an
equestrian sport similar to polo.

Ahmed fathered nine sons and four daughters with his two
wives, Mahfiruz Sultan (*d.* 1621) and Mahpeyker Kösem Sultan
(*d.* 1651). Three of his sons became sultans, Osman II, Murad
IV (*r.* 1623–40) and Ibrahim (*r.* 1640–48). He also authored a
collection of poetry, or *divan*, under the pen-name of Bahti.